To the master of Chinese Charades
10/96

THE I CHING 易經

ASIAPAC COMIC SERIES

THE I CHING 易經

An Illustrated Guide to the Chinese Art of Divination

Illustrated by **Tan Xiaochun**
Translated by **Koh Kok Kiang**

ASIAPAC. SINGAPORE

Publisher
ASIAPAC BOOKS PTE LTD
629 Aljunied Road
#04-06 Cititech Industrial Building
Singapore 1438
Tel: 7453868
Fax: 7453822

First published September 1993
Revised edition December 1993
Reprinted June 1994

ISBN 981-3029-07-2

Cover design by Virus Art
Typeset by Quaser Technology Private Limited
Body text in 8/9 pt Helvetica
Printed in Singapore by Loi Printing Pte Ltd

Publisher's Note

Since the publication of the first edition of *The I Ching*, we have received warm responses towards the contents covered in this title. In particular, many readers who carefully follow the steps in the Yarrow Stalk Method have expressed the wish for a faster way to inquiry through the I Ching. To meet this need, we have included in this revised edition additional divination methods that have proven popular, including the Three Coins Method, the Eight Coins Method, the Pebble Method and the Method of Sixteen.

Besides, other useful features are also appended: divination guidelines, the hexagram chart, and a brief chronology of Chinese history to help readers to place historical events in their proper context.

According to traditions, the imprisoned Marquis Ji Chang used his divination manual, a revision of the *Book of Changes* handed down from his predecessors, and overthrew the despotic King Zhou of the Shang Dynasty. Later, Ji Chang became King Wen of the Zhou Dynasty, whilst his work became known as the *Zhou Yi*. Since then, warring leaders in old China have sought wisdom and guidance from the *Zhou Yi* (now commonly called the I Ching) before taking military action. Its logic has also influenced the philosophy of great sages such as Confucius and Lao Zi.

In this introductory volume, we aim to introduce and explain the theory of the I Ching to readers. You will appreciate the simple yet comprehensive way in which the origin and logic of the I Ching are explained using cartoons.

Subsequent to this volume is a book which will tell more stories related to the history of the I Ching.

We feel honoured to have the cartoonist Tan Xiaochun's permission to the translation rights for his comics. We also like to thank Mr Koh Kok Kiang for translating this volume and writing the Introduction, and the production team for putting in their best effort in the publication of this book.

About the Illustrator

Tan Xiaochun was born in 1949 in the city of Wuhan in Hubei province in China.

In 1957, his family moved to Beijing, the capital of China. While in high school, his interests were varied. However, he was especially fond of mathematics, physics, literature and philosophy. He graduated from the Tianjin Art Institute in 1977. Since then, he has been involved in the production of picture story books.

He feels that the I Ching epitomizes the essence of ancient Oriental wisdom and modern Occidental scientific research. Hence, he has decided to present it in the form of cartoons.

At present he works as an editor in the People's Fine Arts Publishing House. Tan is also a member of various art associations and organizations specializing in I Ching research.

About the Translator

Koh Kok Kiang is a journalist by vocation and a quietist by inclination. His interest in cultural topics and things of the mind started in his schooling years. It is his wish to discover the wisdom of the East that has kindled his interest in Eastern philosophy. He has also translated other titles in Asiapac Comic Series, namely *Book of Zen, Origins of Zen, Sayings of Lie Zi, Sayings of Lao Zi, Sayings of Lao Zi 2, Sayings of Zhuang Zi 2, Roots of Wisdom* and *Thirty-six Stratagems.*

Introduction

The I Ching is without doubt the most influential book in the whole of Chinese civilization. Since it first appeared in its most basic form about three thousand years ago, it has expanded its influence from the nobility, who were the first to consult it, to people from all walks of life. The influence of the I Ching later spread beyond China to other civilizations in the Far East, where it is still in regular use. Indeed, more uses for the I Ching have been found with the passage of time. In the modern era, the I Ching inspired the invention of binary mathematics, the theoretical ancestor of computer language, and its 64 hexagrams have been shown to correspond to the 64 codons of the DNA, the genetic code of life. And in our business-oriented world, the I Ching has been said to be able to predict the stock market.

It is thus clear that through the ages the I Ching has come to mean different things to different people. The I Ching has universal appeal because the human mind is basically the same everywhere, and its use is limited only by one's own powers of perception:

– To the countless millions of people who consult it, the I Ching is a reliable book of divination for the important issues of life.

– To Confucius, one of the most influential thinkers in world history, it was a source of ethics.

– To the Taoists and Buddhists, it is a means of predicting one's conduct and a guide to living rightly to avoid unnecessary suffering and a tragic fate.

– To Gottfried Wilhelm von Leibniz, the eighteenth century scientist who invented calculus, it was the essence of binary mathematics.

– To Carl Gustav Jung, the rival of Sigmund Freud in psychology, it was an explorer of the unconscious mind.

– To some Wall Street executives, according to Adam Smith in his book *Powers of Mind* (Random House, New York, 1975), it can predict stock market movements.

Throughout Chinese history, different people such as Confucius, Taoists, political and military strategists, and fortune-tellers have given varied interpretations of the significance of the I Ching. Are they all wrong or are they all right , or are some wrong and some right? In the grand tradition of the I Ching, what one makes of the I Ching is up to one's mental and spiritual capacity. In philosophical terms, since the Tao includes everything (all is one, one is all), everything is valid so long as it is the truth.

The I Ching has certainly come a long way from its initial usage as a book of oracles. It has become the dominant influence in Chinese folk culture and still touches the daily lives of millions of people through its role in astrology, geomancy, life-nurturing practices, medical theory and fortune-telling.

The influence of the I Ching has gone beyond Chinese culture and it is thus not surprising that of all the Chinese classics, the I Ching is the one that is most widely known and widely translated in the West. More than thirty versions are in print in the English language. Most of them focus on the I Ching as a book of divination. They are popular titles targeted at the mass market. Some are works of scholarship (for example, *Rediscovering the I Ching* by Greg Whincup) which claim that all subsequent additions to the basic text of the I Ching are spurious. For instance, they dismiss the Ten Wings which are commentaries appended by Confucians. The I Ching somehow became part of the Confucian classics in the Han Dynasty when Confucianism became the state ideology and it was required reading for all scholars.

While it is true that many Chinese classics have been corrupted, in the case of the I Ching it can happily co-exist with the interpretations of different minds so long as one shows a genuine interest in it. Therein lies its universal appeal. Some divination methods have gone beyond the original concept of the I Ching into the realm of astrology and yet the users say these methods are just as reliable, if not better than the traditional methods using yarrow stalks or coins. Can one limit the potential of the I Ching?

Three Asian scientists credit the I Ching with helping them to win the Nobel prize for physics. They said they consulted the I Ching in the course of their research. In 1949, Japanese physicist Hideki Yukawa won the prize for his research into the theory of elementary particles. In 1957, Chinese physicists Yang Chen Ning and Lee Tsung Dao shared the award for their studies of particle physics.

Primitive man, awed by the mysteries of nature, believed in a power behind all things and events, which worked to a definite but hidden purpose. He communicated with the power through oracles, whose effectiveness was proof of man's importance, and therefore cannot be doubted.

Although man's belief later became more sophisticated with scientific progress, his needs remain the same. He does not openly believe in the supernatural because that flies in the face of science in which theories are logically explained. But neither does he want to deny it outright. How then can he maintain intellectual honesty? There are two ways.

One way, which Confucius followed as a matter of principle, was not to address such questions. When asked whether the spirits of one's ancestors actually came to partake of ritual offerings, he said: "You would be unenlightened to think that they actually came, and unkind to think that they did not."

Another way, which amounts to the same thing, is to say with the famous physicist Niels Bohr, when confronted with the incongruity that a great scientist like him should hang a horseshoe over his door, "I understand that it works even if you don't believe in it."

So how does the I Ching work?

The basic premise at the root of the I Ching is that cosmic order and human nature are one. Divination by various methods is a means of stopping time to see the changes that are in progress at a given time. Thus one can align oneself with these changes, going with one's Tao instead of fighting vainly against it, and discovering one's nature in the process.

Consulting the I Ching is one of the most straightforward, objective and least "psychic" of all forms of divination, requiring no special skill or aptitude for clairvoyance.

Most of the information on the history of the I Ching in this comic version comes from the Song Dynasty edition of Zhu Xi, a prominent Neo-Confucian scholar.

Koh Kok Kiang

Contents

Appendices

Origins of the I Ching *

易经的产生

* The I Ching is also known as the *Zhou Yi*.

1
In ancient times,
Fu Xi
ruled the world.
2
He often
looked up to observe
heavenly
phenomena...
3
... and
gazed down
to examine
earthly contours.
4
He also observed
the markings of
birds and beasts
and how they fit
into their habitats.
5
He studied plant life in
all forms and investigated
the mysterious workings
of nature.

Not only did Fu Xi observed the phenomena around him, but he also carefully noted deliberate bodily movements and the changes they brought about.

7

He believed that whether it was outward phenomena or one's own movements, they followed a common law of existence. He was determined to find out what that law of existence was.

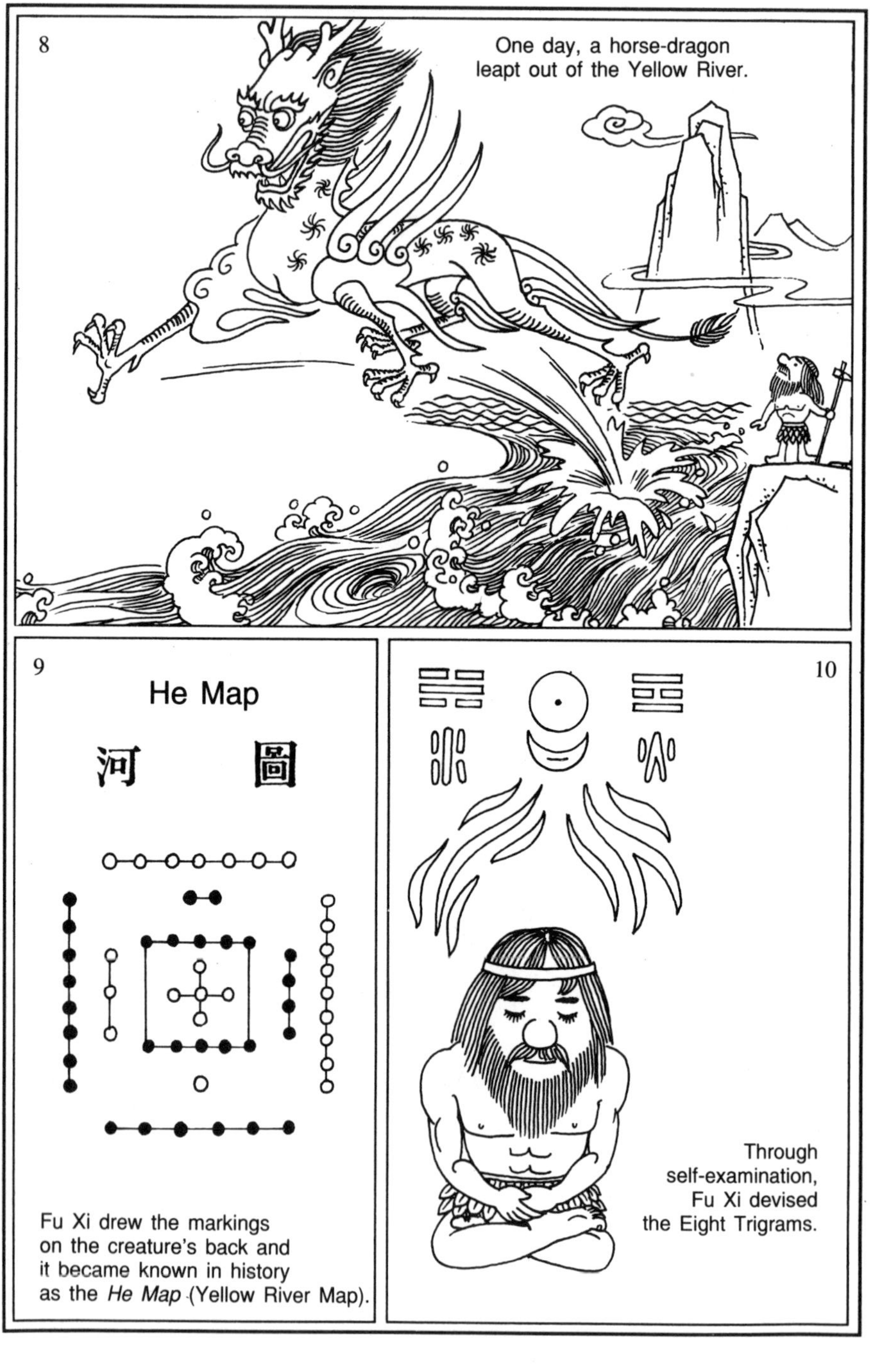

8

One day, a horse-dragon leapt out of the Yellow River.

9

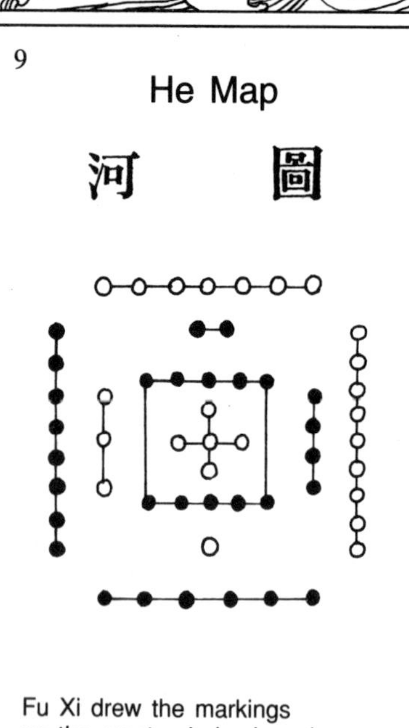

Fu Xi drew the markings on the creature's back and it became known in history as the *He Map* (Yellow River Map).

10

11
Because the Eight Trigrams are derived from the patterns and changes of nature, they reflect the laws of the universe.
12
Hence people can derive illuminating guidance from it.
13
It can help people act rightly to avoid harm.

14
After Fu Xi came Shen Nong. He invented the plough and introduced agriculture. He got the idea from the hexagram Yi.
HEXAGRAM YI
Ooo
15
Shen Nong was followed by the Yellow Emperor...
16
... and Yao...
17
HEXAGRAM HUAN
... and Shun and others. During their time, they taught the world how to make boats. They got this idea from the hexagram Huan. They understood the Eight Trigrams and benefited the people. These rulers enjoyed popular support and it was as if they had divine help.

20

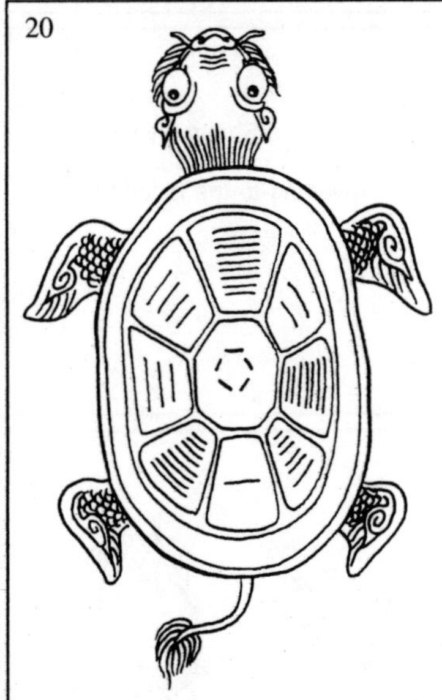

On its shell were some markings, which looked like a form of writing.

21

Luo Map

洛 書

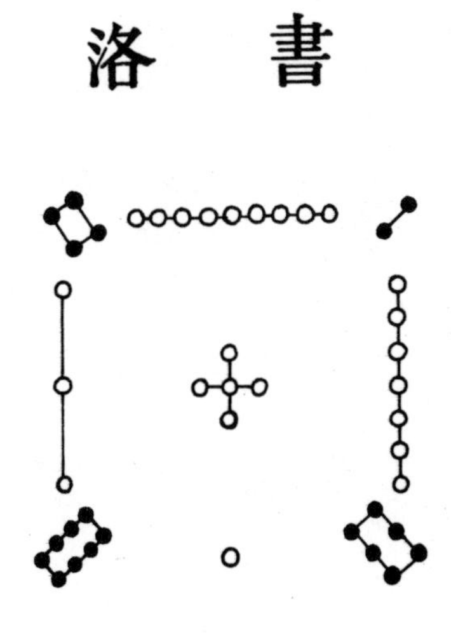

Yu the Great wrote it down and it later came to be known as the *Luo Map*.

22

Talented people used the Eight Trigrams to form 64 hexagrams.

23

Over the years, the trigrams evolved into their present form. During the Xia Dynasty it was known as *Lian Shan* (or "mountains standing together").

24

At the time of the Shang Dynasty it was called *Gui Cang* (or "reverting to the hidden").

25

... and during the Zhou Dynasty it was known as *Zhou Yi* (or "changes of Zhou").

26

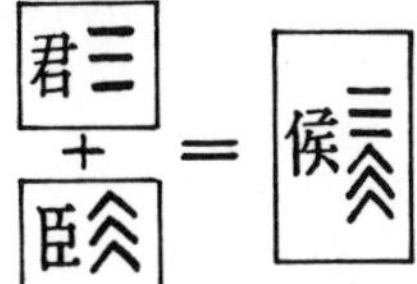

They were the *Three Ancient Books of Changes*. Although their symbols, terminology, and sequence of hexagrams were different, they were all the product of the Eight Trigrams. *Lian Shan* and *Gui Cang* are now lost.

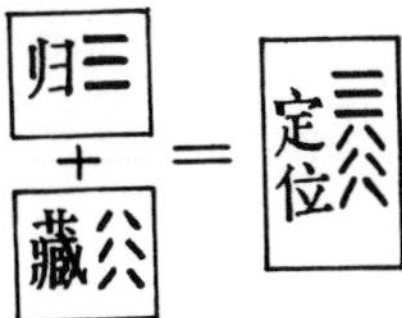

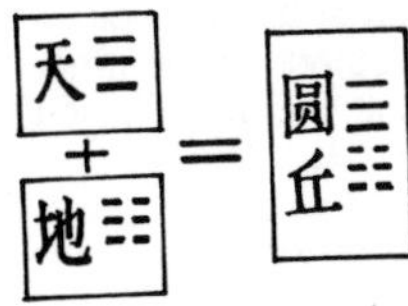

27

28

29

Ji Chang spent his time studying the *Book of Changes* and understood it profoundly.

30

He incorporated his findings into the divination methods of his predecessors and the result was a divination manual.

After his release, he recovered his lost territories and later became King Wen of the Zhou Dynasty. The work, which he wrote in prison, became known as the *Zhou Yi*.

31

32

Since then, people have regarded the *Zhou Yi* as being based on divine principles because it includes the laws of transformation of things and events. It was revered as a classic.

33

Educated people were fond of spending their leisure looking at the hexagrams and pondering over them to understand the underlying mystery.

34

師

Before taking actions, generals often consulted the hexagrams to find out what fate had in store for them based on their tendencies.

35

Hence they did not act in the usual manner but adopted the words of the hexagrams as a guide. This was like receiving divine help and success seemed assured.

36

Confucius had a deep understanding of the *Zhou Yi*. In his later years, he always had it at hand. He said:

37

He handled his copy of the *Zhou Yi* so often that the binding came apart three times.

Confucius and other scholars of the Spring and Autumn and Warring States periods wrote commentaries on the *Zhou Yi*. Ten of the most famous works were known collectively as the *Zhou Treatise*.

39

The *Zhou Yi* itself became elevated to the status of a classic, hence it is also known as the *Classic of Changes*. For some two thousand years, it was part of the *Five Classics* of Confucianism and was required reading for scholars.

Mysterious Book for All Times

1

Lao Zi, the founder of Taoism, said: "The Tao that embraces all things cannot be easily expressed in words."

2

Confucius said: "Words cannot convey the depth of language, and language cannot convey the depth of meaning."

3

If this is so, does it mean that the understanding of Fu Xi, King Wen, and other sages cannot be communicated to others?

It was precisely because of the limitations of language that the sages resorted to using abstract symbols to convey meanings.

4

5

They used symbols such as the trigrams, which could represent opposites, to express their thinking.

6

The sages foresaw that people might not be able to understand what the symbols meant. Therefore they added some script to explain the hexagrams.

7

8

If one does not confine oneself to just the literal meaning of the words but learn to read between the lines, one will perceive the underlying wisdom.

10

12

Its elegant hexagrams, profound script, ability to influence the outcome of events, and precise mathematical structure make the *Zhou Yi* a unique classic for all times.

13 Famous thinkers and philosophers in Chinese history have benefited from the *Zhou Yi*.

14 Those who sought to establish themselves never failed to rely on the guidance of the *Zhou Yi*.

Li Jing, a famous general who helped establish the Tang dynasty.

Zhuge Liang, a great strategist of the Three Kingdoms period.

Zhang Liang, a famous strategist who played a key role in the founding of the Han dynasty.

Jiang Ziya, a strategist who helped establish the Zhou dynasty.

15

Scientists can find parallels between the hexagrams and scientific formulae.

German mathematician Gottfried Wilhelm von Leibniz (1646-1716), inspired by the Eight Trigrams, perfected the binary system of numeration and invented integral and differential calculus, which are the theoretical ancestor of modern computers.

16

Martin Schonberger, in his book *The Hidden Key to Life*, noted that the 64 hexagrams of the I Ching correspond exactly to the 64 DNA codons, the genetic code of life.

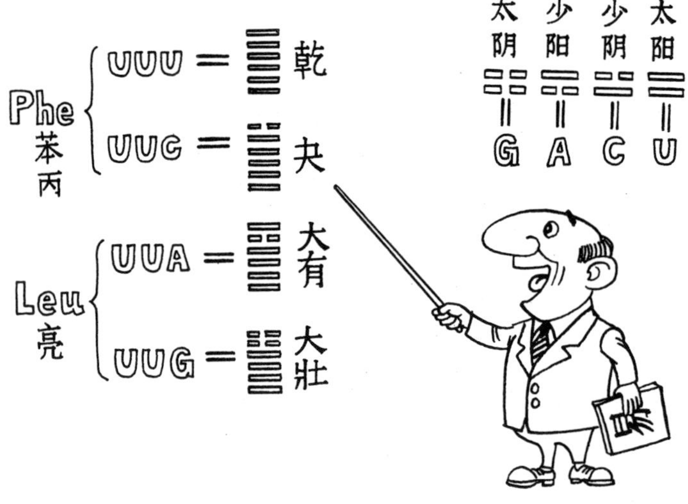

17

Those who believe in divination can use the *Zhou Yi* for fortune-telling.

18 In using the *Zhou Yi*, "the benevolent see benevolence and the wise see wisdom".

South Korean national flag.

Danish physicist Niels Henrik David Bohr (1885-1962).

American physicist Albert Einstein (1879-1955).

19 The *Zhou Yi* is the fountainhead of Chinese culture and has widespread influence.

20 From the whole to the part.

21

We are living in an age of scientific advancement and the *Zhou Yi* remains a gem that will benefit all sectors of society, including the fields of human anatomy, cybernetics, systematics, information theory, quantum theory, dissipation structure theory, and the study of meridians in the body.

Logic of the I Ching

易理

1
All things and events grow and develop unceasingly.
2
Even things made of rock will decay and are not everlasting.
3
What is behind all these changes?
4
The sun and the moon complement each other to give us light.

6

All things and events have opposite states.

7

During the day we see the sun.

9

The succession of opposite states holds a lesson for humanity.

10

The two opposites are called "Yin" and "Yang".

11

According to the Yin-Yang School, Yang corresponds to what is masculine, active, creative, bright, and hard. Symbols of Yang are the sun, fire, the dragon, the colour red, the south, mercury, and all odd numbers.
Yin is the feminine, the passive, the receptive, the soft and the dark. Symbols of Yin are the moon, water, clouds, the tiger, the turtle, the colour black, the north, lead, and all even numbers.
The interaction of Yin and Yang gives rise to all changes.

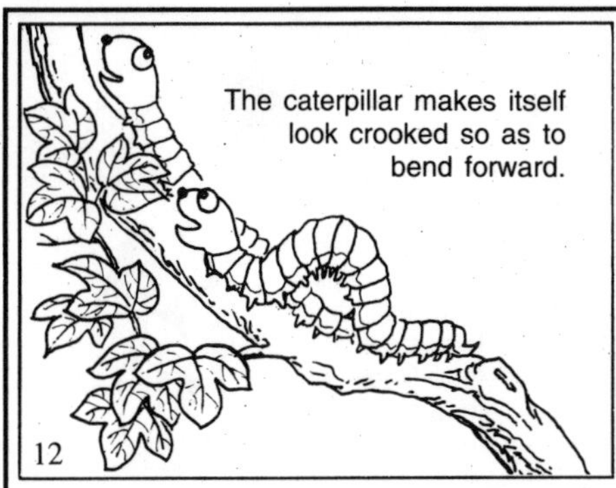
The caterpillar makes itself look crooked so as to bend forward.
12

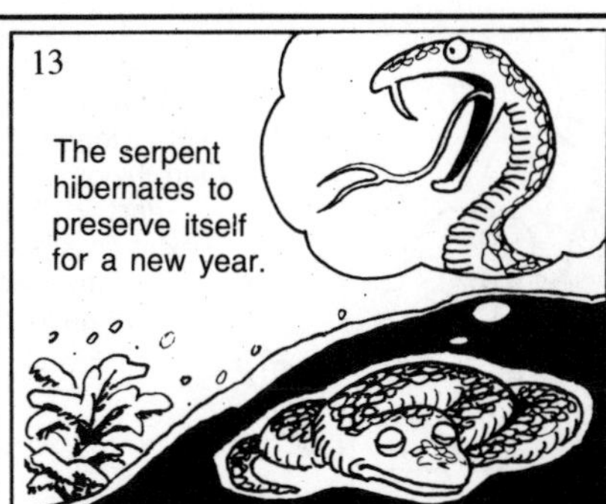
13
The serpent hibernates to preserve itself for a new year.

14
Defence is often to wait for a chance to attack, and attack is often the best form of defence.

15
You're too much!
See you in court!
Yin and Yang are not merely opposite states but can be complementary in nature. This is called the unity of opposites.

16

After noon, the sun starts to set in the west. When things have reached their extreme stage, they start to decline.

17

When the moon is full, it begins to wane. When things are at their fullest stage, they also start to wane.

18

Even day and night must take turns to change with time and circumstances, how much more must man!

19

If one knows only how to move forward and not backward, he will reach a dead end.

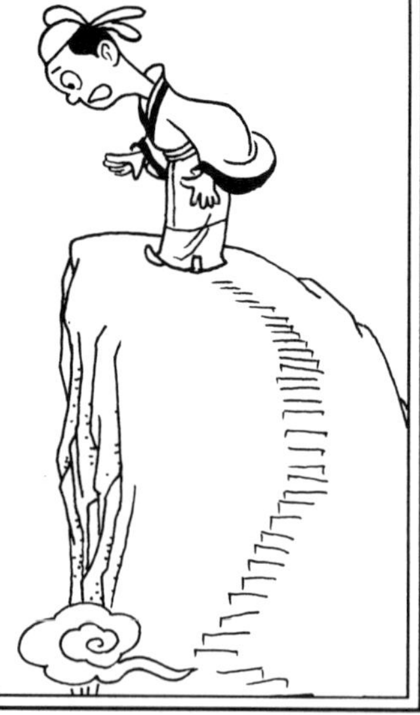

20

If one thinks only of living and ignores risks to life, regret will be too late.

If one thinks only of gain and ignores the possibility of failure, he will run into trouble.

21

22 One who understands the principle of "when at their utmost, things decline" can be said to be a man of insight who comes and goes freely.

23

Once there was a prosperous state, Yin, whose ruler Hai Ke was conceited and vain. The state of Yi was his neighbour.

24

Later, he was killed by the Yi ruler. His state was plundered. Happiness turned into sorrow.

25

Enemy forces from Yi invaded his state and the people fled in terror.

26

27

Sorrow and happiness, poverty and wealth, Yin and Yang will transform from one into the other under certain conditions.

28
Ice three feet thick is not due to one day's cold.
The transformation of things begin at a certain stage. When things have reached a certain limit, change is inevitable.
29
Some good deeds may seem insignificant.
$
30
But many small deeds add up to a good name.
31
If one dismisses small acts of charity...

32

... and disregards his little faults...

33

... he will end up committing grave errors and be beyond help.

34

If water only flows and is not accumulated, or flows faster than it is accumulated, then the river will dry up.

35

But if water is accumulated and does not flow or does not flow fast enough, then the dam will burst.

36
Overaccumulation and overflow are both not good. It is best to have a balance so that the flow of water can be controlled.
37
If things are kept within reasonable bounds and the balance of Yin and Yang is maintained, then they will last.
38
When Yin and Yang are in balance, this is called "the middle way".

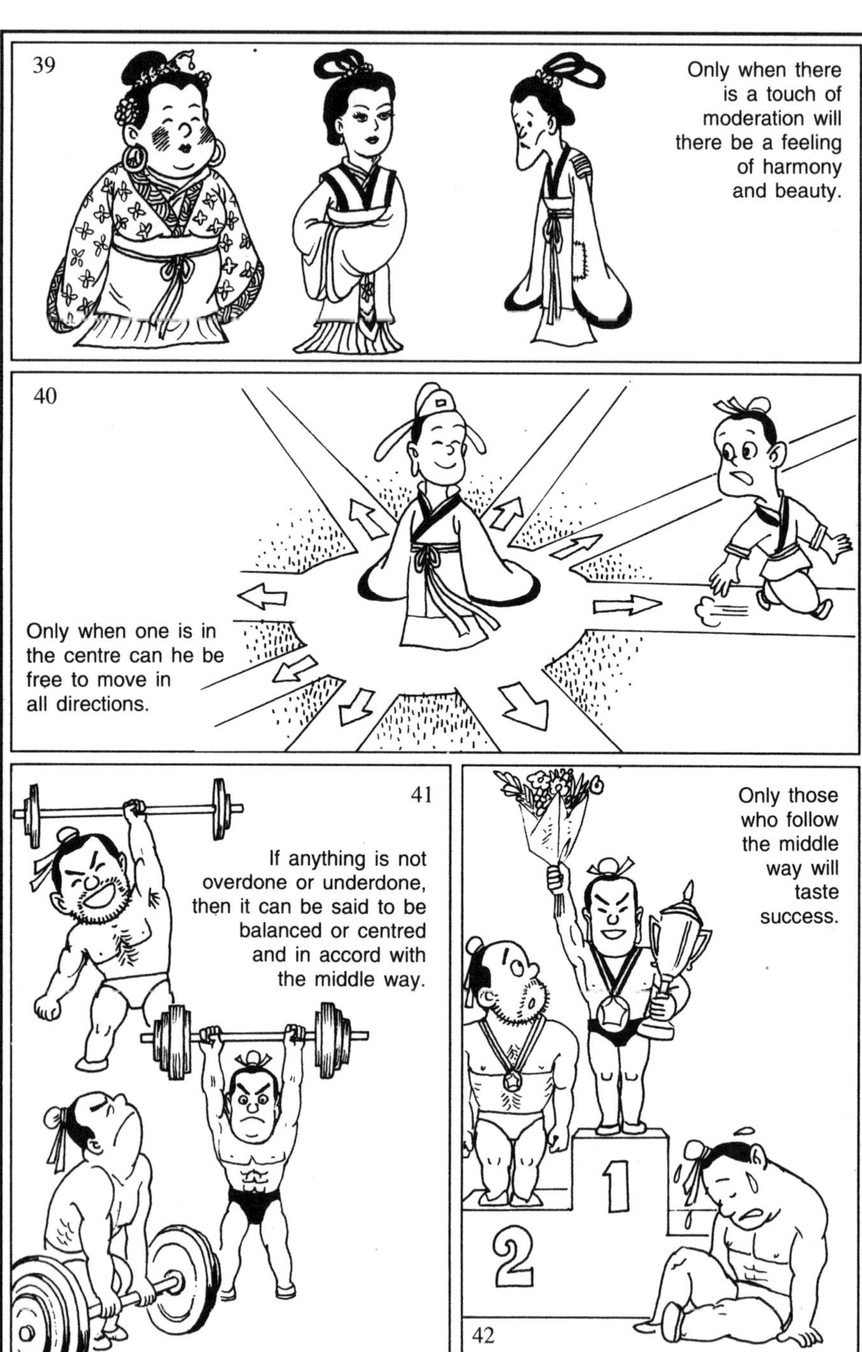
39
Only when there is a touch of moderation will there be a feeling of harmony and beauty.
40
Only when one is in the centre can he be free to move in all directions.
41
If anything is not overdone or underdone, then it can be said to be balanced or centred and in accord with the middle way.
Only those who follow the middle way will taste success.
1
2
42

43
The development of events often upsets the balance of Yin and Yang and strays beyond the middle way.
44
As long as it is not too serious, it can be rectified although it calls for a greater than usual effort.
Only when "the crooked is made straight" will the wrongdoer return to the middle way.
45
46
Balance is like steering a vehicle. One must constantly turn right or left so that the car can make steady progress along the road.

47

The thief does not regard theft as shameful.

48

The bandit does not regard plunder as wicked.

49

To punish them is to prevent them from committing worse offences.

50

Such punishment can be said to have saved them and can be regarded as a blessing.

51

52

War to the victor is glory, but to the vanquished it is a curse.

53

In the victorious nation, the one who enjoys the spoils of war is the triumphant general.

54

But to the ordinary soldiers who lost their lives on the battlefield, what glory is there to speak of?

55

When people judge things, they do so from a fixed viewpoint. Hence there are opposite views. But there is something that is beyond words, can be one or the other, and in which Yin and Yang are not differentiated. This is the peerless Taiji (Absolute or Supreme Ultimate).

Structure of the I Ching

易象

1

The oneness of Yin and Yang is the Absolute. All things or events are the result of Yin and Yang, hence it can be said that...

All things or events can be said to be part of the Absolute.

2

Up above the universe is the Absolute in big form.

3

Down below a speck of dust is the Absolute in small form.

4

The sum total of the past, present, and future is time in its big Absolute state.

7

The Absolute when differentiated is Yin-Yang, which are called the two states.

8

The unity of Yin-Yang can be split into Yin and Yang.

9

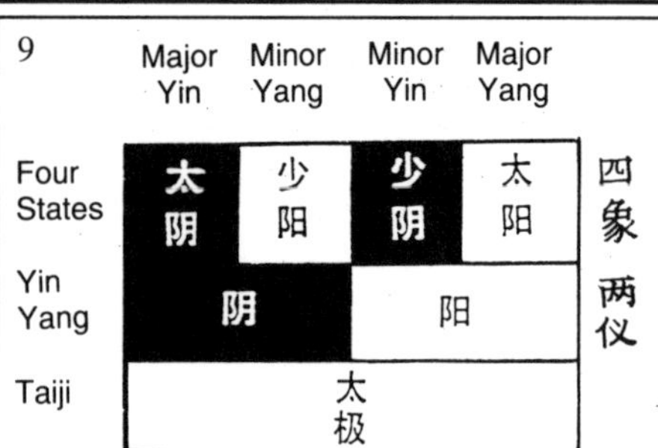

When the Absolute is differentiated twice, there are four forms called the "four states". Of the four states, under Yang are the Major Yang and the Minor Yin, and under Yin are the Major Yin and the Minor Yang.

10

When the four states are further subdivided, they become the Eight Trigrams.

11

The Sequence of Fu Xi's Eight Trigrams

伏羲八卦次序

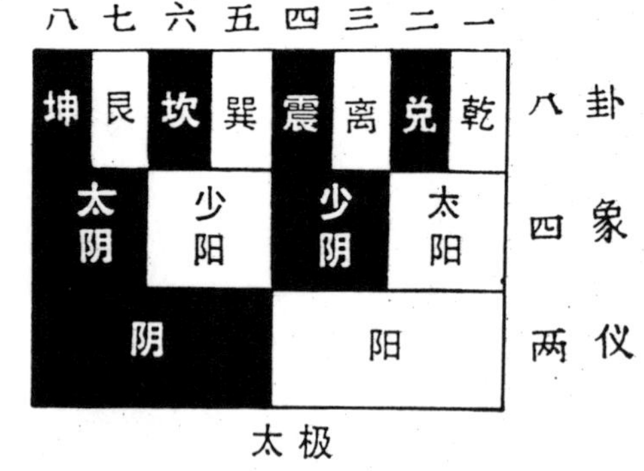

12

Symbols are used to represent Yin and Yang in the *Zhou Yi*. The symbol is called "line".

13 The Eight Trigrams consist of three full and three broken lines and their possible combinations.

Symbol	☰	☱	☲	☳
Name	乾 Qian	兑 Dui	离 Li	震 Zhen
Order	一 1	二 2	三 3	四 4
Symbol	☴	☵	☶	☷
Name	巽 Xun	坎 Kan	艮 Gen	坤 Kun
Order	五 5	六 6	七 7	八 8

14 To make it easy to remember the Eight Trigrams, a mnemonic was devised:

Qian three full, Kun three broken,
Zhen open bowl, Gen inverted bowl,
Li empty middle, Kan full middle,
Dui deficient top, Xun broken bottom.

15

When the Eight Trigrams are further subdivided three times, we get Fu Xi's 64 hexagrams. It is easy to understand this: When the Absolute is subdivided six times, we get 64 hexagrams. And the combinations of the trigrams result in 64 hexagrams.

The Sequence of Fu Xi's 64 Hexagrams

伏 羲 六 十 四 卦 次 序

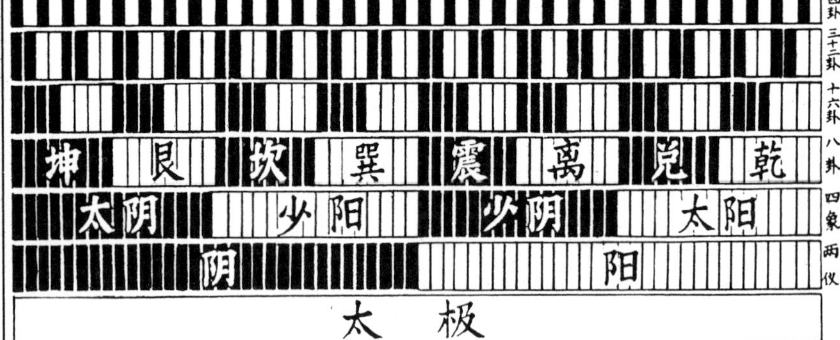

16

The six lines of the hexagram are built up from bottom to top and are called:

17 The first line represents the beginning of things.

First Line.

Top line.

18 The top line represents the end of things.

?

The first line is likened to a tree's roots, which are not easily identified.

19

20

The top line is likened to the foliage, which is easy to perceive.

21

To understand a matter in its entirety, we need to consider the matter from its first line (beginning) to its top line (end).

22

Since the Absolute covers all things, we must first find out the Yin and Yang aspects of things.

23
With Qian and Kun as the extremes of Yang and Yin, it is easy to see which is which.
It is not bad to be shorter than him.
It is also not bad to be taller than him.
24
The Yin and Yang aspects of the Absolute combine to give things their characteristics and their place within different categories.

25 Many things undergo transformation according to a law of change. One complete cycle of cold and heat is the Absolute. For example, the succession of the seasons.

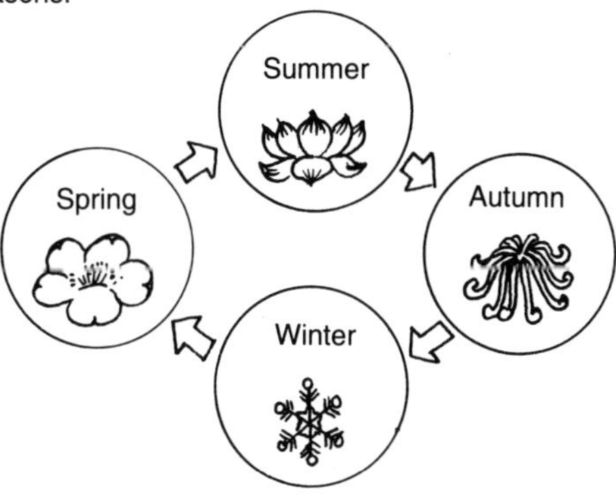

26

Fu Xi's Eight Trigrams Chart

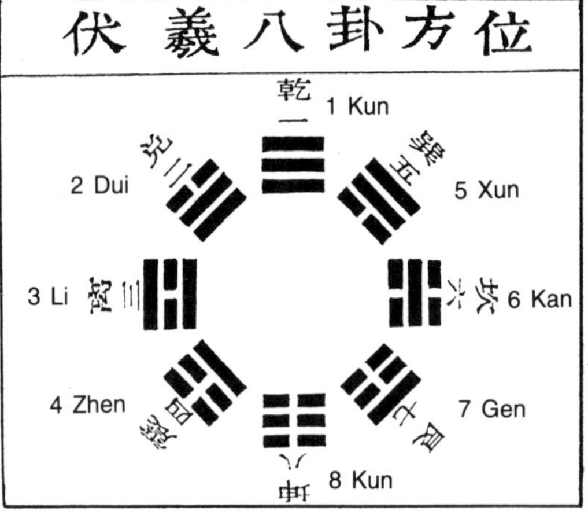

In the second year, the pattern of the seasons is repeated. Hence the Eight Trigrams are arranged in a cyclical pattern. This is called "Fu Xi's Circular Arrangement of the Trigrams in Pairs of Opposites".

27

Cyclical Chart of the 64 Hexagrams

六十四卦圆图

If we develop this further, we get a “Cyclical Chart of the 64 Hexagrams”. Because the changes under heaven are also cyclical in nature, the chart is also called the “Heavenly Cyclical Chart”.

The hexagrams can also be arranged in the shape of a square, giving rise to the "Earthly Square Chart of the 64 Hexagrams". The chart has Qian at the bottom and the sequence ends with Kun at the top.

Earthly Square Chart of the 64 Hexagrams

Kun	Gen	Kan	Xun	Zhen	Li	Dui	Qian	Upper Trigram / Lower Trigram
Kun	Bo	Bi	Guan	Yü	Jin	Cui	Pi	Kun
Qian	Gen	Jian	Jian	Xiao Guo	Lü	Xian	Dun	Gen
Shi	Meng	Kan	Huan	Jie	Wei Ji	Kun	Song	Kan
Sheng	Gu	Jing	Xun	Heng	Ding	Da Guo	Gou	Xun
Fu	Yi	Tun	Yi	Zhen	Shi Ke	Sui	Wu Wang	Zhen
Ming Yi	Bi	Ji Ji	Jia Ren	Feng	Li	Ge	Tong Ren	Li
Lin	Sun	Jie	Zhong Fu	Gui Mei	Kui	Dui	Lü	Dui
Tai	Da Chu	Xu	Xiao Chu	Da Zhuang	Da You	Guai	Qian	Qian

29

The Position of the 64 Hexagrams

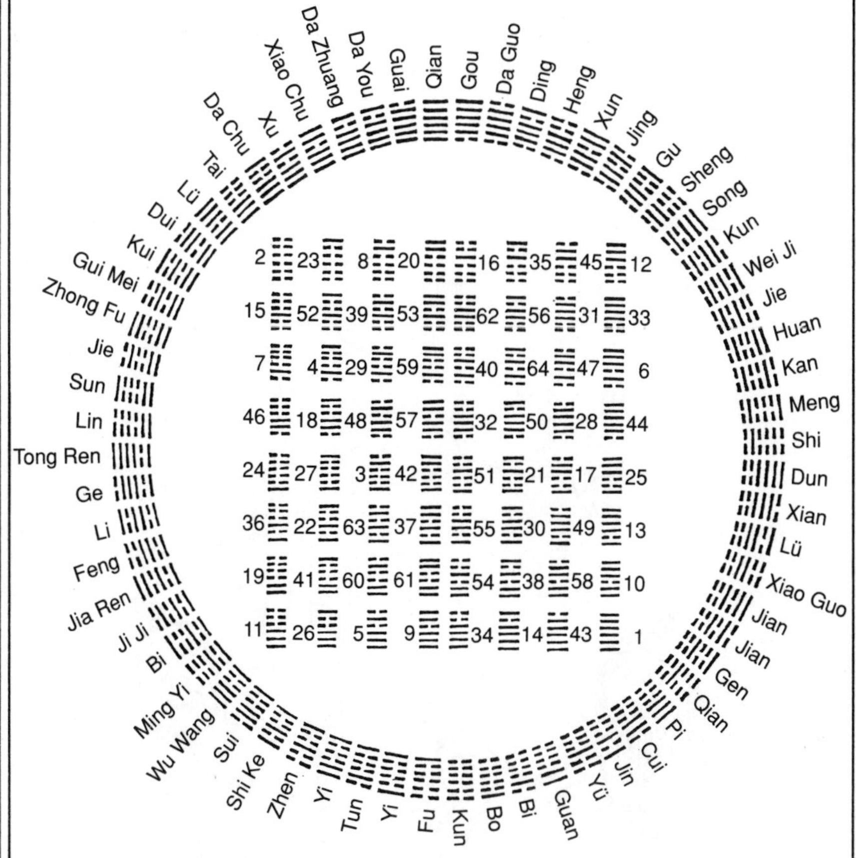

When the round and square charts are combined, we get "Fu Xi's Chart of the Structure of the 64 Hexagrams". The whole thing is called the "Earlier Heaven I Ching". It shows the relationship of the combination of Yin and Yang in the hexagrams.

*Indicated in the square chart are the hexagram numbers.

30

The study of the attributes and relationships of the hexagrams is called "Later Heaven I Ching". It was said to be named in honour of King Wen and is also called the "Wen Wang".

31

If the characteristics of the Eight Trigrams are represented by a family:

乾

Qian is hard, represented by the father.

坤

Kun is soft, represented by the mother.

The other six trigrams represent the sons and daughters.

离

Li

巽

Xun

坎

Kan

震

Zhen

32

King Wen's Sequence of the Eight Trigrams

文王八卦次序

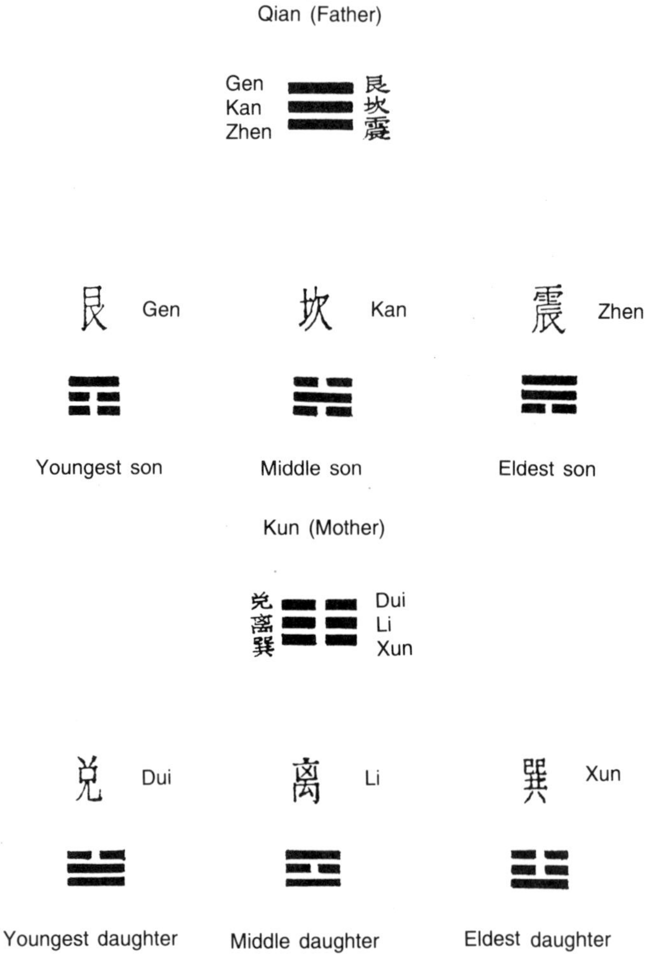

Qian (Father)

Gen 艮
Kan 坎
Zhen 震

艮 Gen	坎 Kan	震 Zhen
Youngest son	Middle son	Eldest son

Kun (Mother)

兑 Dui
离 Li
巽 Xun

兑 Dui	离 Li	巽 Xun
Youngest daughter	Middle daughter	Eldest daughter

33 If we use creatures to represent the characteristics of the Eight Trigrams:

Qian represents vigour, like a horse.

Kun represents docility, like cattle.

Zhen represents thunderbolt, like a dragon.

Xun represents a submissive role, like a chicken.

Kan represents being at the bottom, like a pig under splashing water.

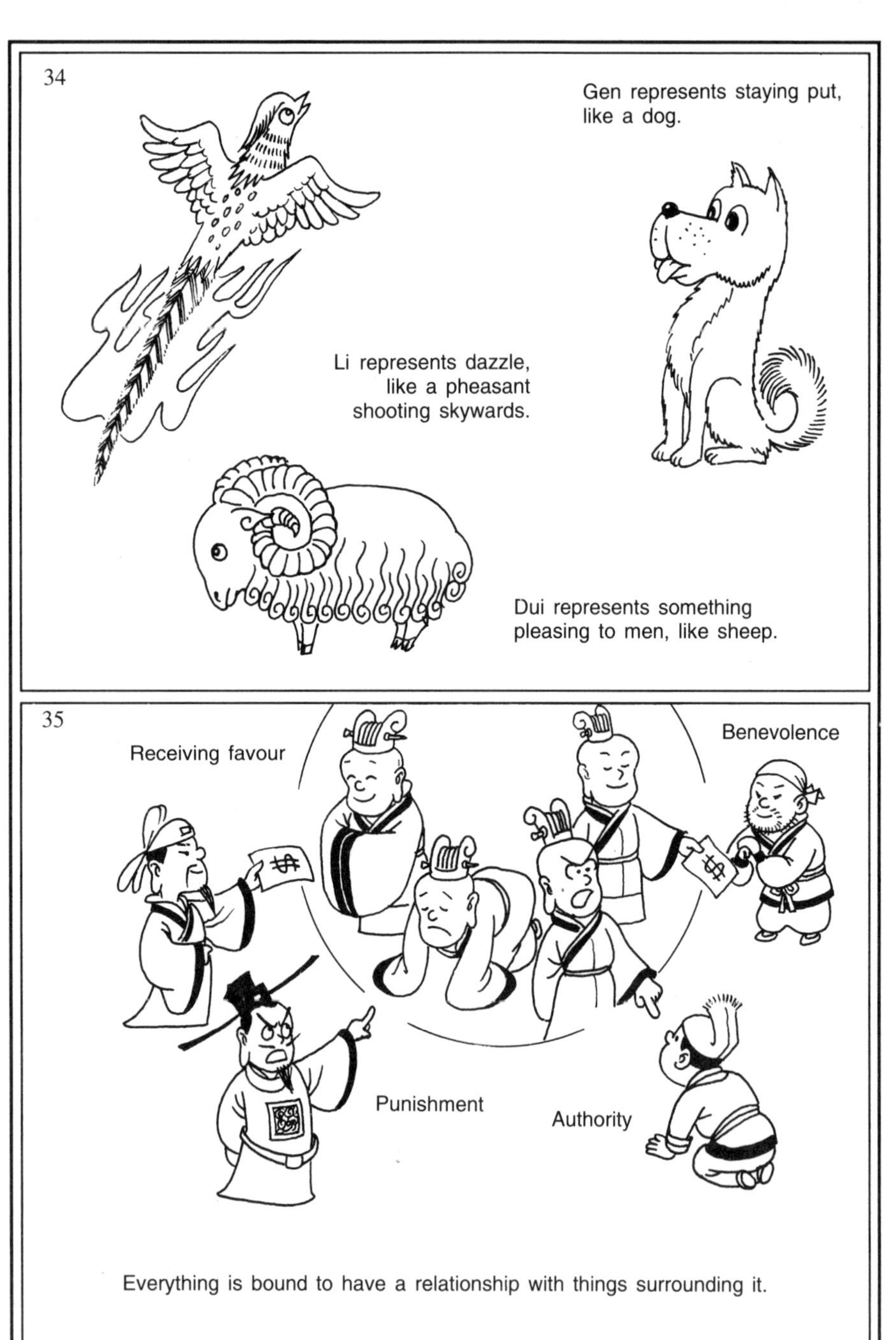
34
Gen represents staying put, like a dog.
Li represents dazzle, like a pheasant shooting skywards.
Dui represents something pleasing to men, like sheep.
35
Receiving favour
Benevolence
Punishment
Authority
Everything is bound to have a relationship with things surrounding it.

36 Chart of Life Links and the Five Elements

五行生克图

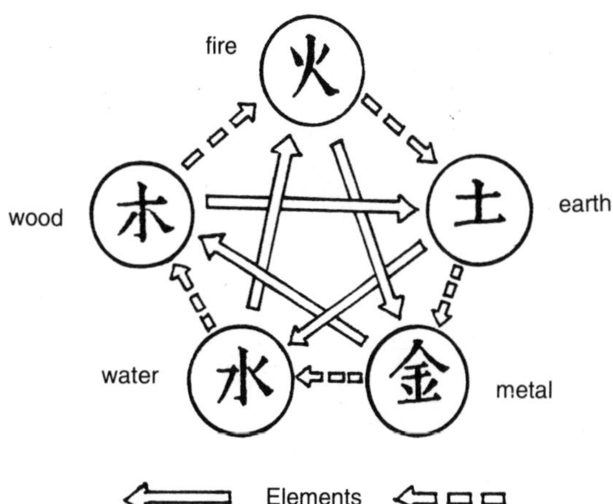

In the old days, relationships between things were known as "Life Links". Metal, water, wood, fire, and earth were called the "Five Elements". They reflected the dynamic relationships between things.

37

When the Five Elements and Life Links are missing, the order of things will be reversed.

If not for me, who will feed you?

38 The Eight Trigrams and the Five Elements balance one another in the following way:

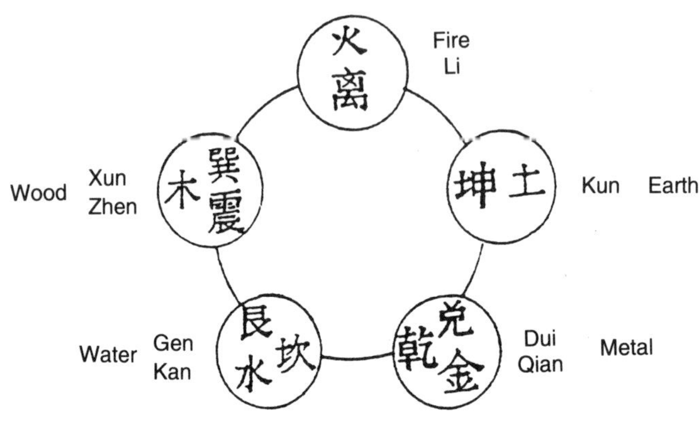

39

King Wen's Circular Arrangement of the Trigrams

文王八卦方位

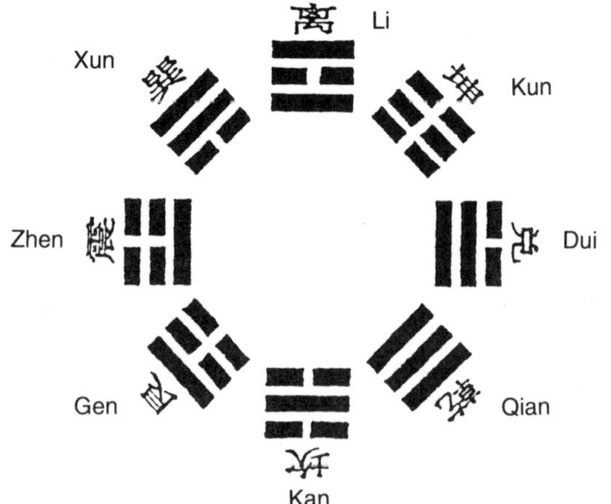

40

The Eight Trigrams match the Eight Directions, the Four Seasons, and the Five Elements to give:

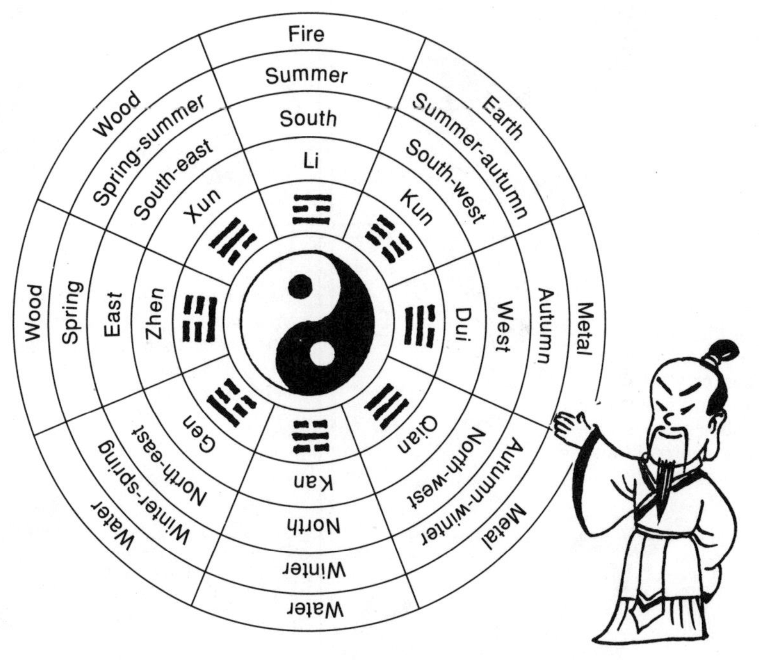

41
The nature of Zhen is movement. It is like thunderbolts in spring, and the stirrings of life in spring. Zhen also represents thunder.
42
The nature of Xun is going into. It is like the wind carrying a kite into the sky. It depicts life thriving and its time is the passing of spring into summer. Xun also represents wind.
43
The nature of Li is attachment. It is like the fire which can only consume in the presence of a substance. Its time is summer. Li also represents fire.
44
The nature of Kun is submission. It is like the earth supporting the firmament. Its time is the passing of summer into autumn. Kun also represents earth.

45

The nature of Dui is delight, like the ripening of things. Its time is autumn. Dui represents marsh.

46

The nature of Qian is vigour, like the ever-changing scenes of the firmament. Its time is the passing of autumn into winter. Qian also represents heaven.

47 The nature of Kan is sinking, like creatures going into hibernation in winter. Kan also represents water.

48 The nature of Gen is stopping. Its time is the passing of winter into spring. Gen also represents mountain, which is immovable.

49 Manifestations of the Eight Trigrams.

☱	☶	☲	☵	☴	☳	☷	☰
兑	艮	离	坎	巽	震	坤	乾
Dui	Gen	Li	Kan	Xun	Zhen	Kun	Qian
泽	山	火	水	风	雷	地	天
Marsh	Mountain	Fire	Water	Wind	Thunder	Earth	Heaven

50 The Tao of heaven has Yin and Yang, the Tao of earth has soft and hard, and the Tao of humanity has benevolence and righteousness.

51 The *Zhou Yi* depicts the way of heaven, earth, and man. Hence the six lines form a hexagram.

Way of heaven	天道 <	阴	Yin
		阳	Yang
Way of man	人道 <	仁	Benevolence
		义	Righteousness
Way of earth	地道 <	柔	Soft
		刚	Hard, Strong

52

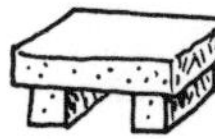

The second, fourth, and sixth lines from the bottom represent Yin. The first, third, and fifth lines represent Yang.

53

When Yang and Yin are in their proper places, this is called "keeping position" and "maintaining correctness". This is auspicious.

54

The two principles enable the hard to stay hard and the soft to stay soft. Otherwise the order of things will be upset.

55

If Yang and Yin usurp one another's position, this is called "losing position" and "no correctness". Most inauspicious.

56

"Losing position" and "no correctness" cause the hard to become soft and the soft to become hard.

57

When Yin and Yang are next to each other in their proper places, this is called "being compatible". Auspicious.

If Yang is next to Yang, and Yin is next to Yin, there is tension. This is called "not being compatible". Fearsome.

58

When the Yang line is above Yin, this is called "Yang rides Yin" and "Yin carries Yang". Favourable.

59

When the Yin line is above the Yang line, this is "Yin rides Yang" and "Yang carries Yin". Terrible.

Family members 家人

Upper trigram 上卦

Lower trigram 下卦

Top line

Fifth line

Fourth line

Third line

Second line

First line

The six lines can be arranged in sets of three with one set above and one set below. They balance one another out. If not, when hard and soft are identical, they have "no correspondence". When hard and soft are differentiated, they "have correspondence".

The I Ching Numerology

易数

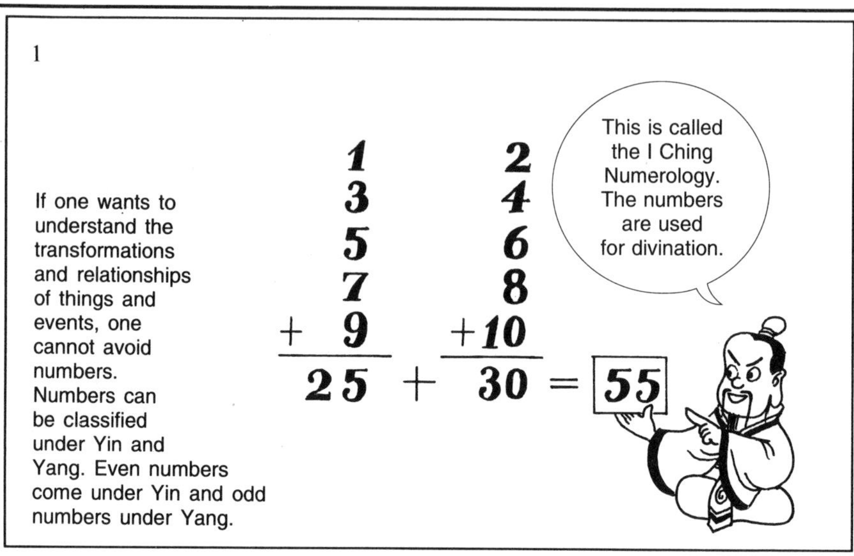

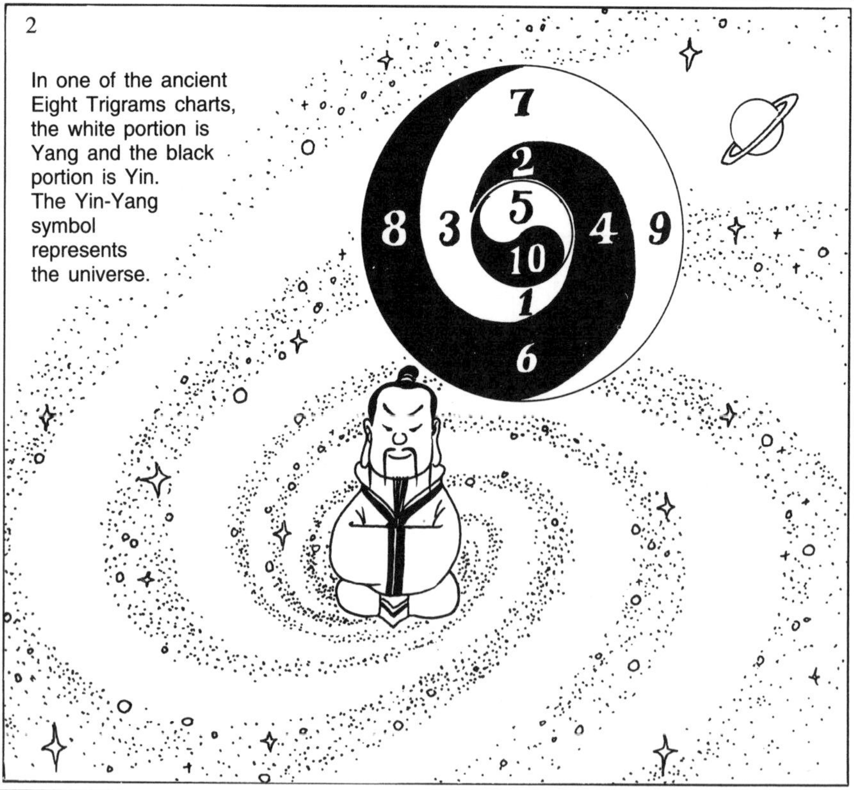

2

In one of the ancient Eight Trigrams charts, the white portion is Yang and the black portion is Yin. The Yin-Yang symbol represents the universe.

7 2 5 8 3 4 9 10 1 6

3

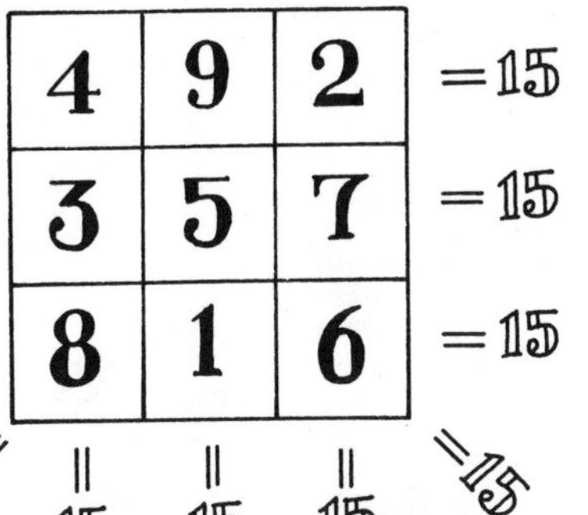

4	9	2	=15
3	5	7	=15
8	1	6	=15
=15	=15	=15	=15

The left diagonal and the right diagonal are each marked =15.

All-round harmony of Yin and Yang and the ideal pattern for things.

One of the charts called the Magic Square of Three arranges numbers such that when they are added up vertically, horizontally, or diagonally, the total is 15.

4

When the numbers are combined with the Eight Trigrams, we see the following result:

巽 Xun 四 4	离 Li 九 9	坤 Kun 二 2
震 Zhen 三 3	中 Middle 五 5	兑 Dui 七 7
艮 Gen 八 8	坎 Kan 一 1	乾 Qian 六 6

5

In the *Zhou Yi*, within the symbols are numbers and within the numbers are symbols. Both originate from nature and reflect the common law of the universe.

6

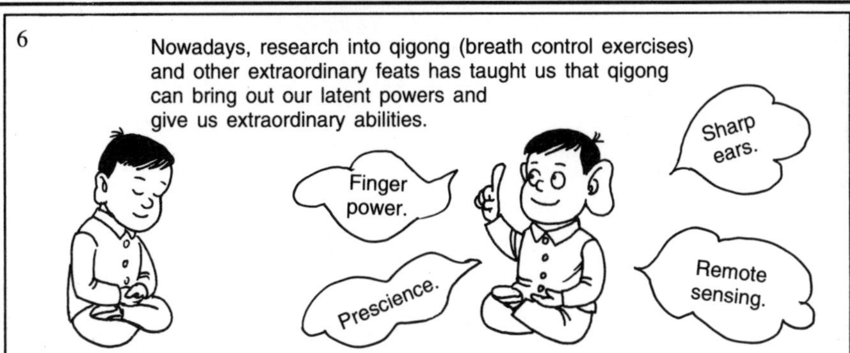

7

In ancient times, there were many qigong masters such as Fu Xi and King Wen who also had other extraordinary powers and achieved many things.

8

From their understanding of life, they devised the hexagrams to benefit the world.

9

The Hexagrams

易卦

1

How to consult the I Ching — Yarrow Stalk Method

2 Find a quiet spot where you will not be disturbed. Relax and collect your mind for a few minutes. Ponder your question and write it down.

3 Based on the I Ching Numerology, 55 stalks are used in divination. Put aside six stalks which represent the six lines of a hexagram. Take the remaining 49 stalks and divide them arbitrarily into two heaps.

4

With any of the heaps, remove one stalk and put it aside.

5

From the same heap, remove four stalks at a time, until 1-4 stalks remain.

6 From the other heap, remove four stalks at a time, until 1-4 stalks remain.

7

Put the stalks (which are in groups of four) in Step 5 and Step 6 together.

8

With this new heap of stalks, divide it randomly into two heaps. Repeat the steps in 4, 5, 6, 7.

9

The above steps are repeated until 6-9 groups of stalks remain. Each group contains four stalks.

Each of these possibilities is assigned a name as follows:

6 — **x** — Old Yin (changing line)
7 ——— Young Yang
8 — — Young Yin
9 — **o** — Old Yang (changing line)

This name obtained constitutes the bottom line of your hexagram.

10

11 Repeat the entire process to build up the other 5 lines of your hexagram. The first three lines form the lower trigram. The next three lines form the upper trigram.

The hexagram in the matter related to your question is obtained when you put the six lines together.

Note:
The numbers 6 and 9 are called changing lines. They change to their opposites: from Yin to Yang, from Old to Young, from solid to broken lines, and vice versa.
When all six lines are unchanging 7's and 8's, the hexagram formed is itself the divination. When one line is a changing 6 or 9, that line is the divination.
When more than one line is a 6 or 9, a second hexagram is formed by changing those lines to the opposite, and the two hexagrams together are the answer to the divination.
For example, by changing the second and fifth lines (both moving lines) in the hexagram,

x

o

(Hexagram 46)

we obtain a second hexagram.

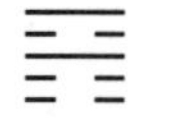

(Hexagram 39)

There is no contradiction in the answer to the divination, for the hexagrams refer to the earlier and later stages of the same event or sequence of events. Between them, they may indicate that the matter will go well (or badly) at first, but that a reversal will occur at a later time.

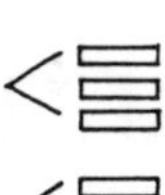

Upper Trigram / Lower Trigram	Qian	Zhen	Kan	Gen	Kun	Xun	Li	Dui
Qian	1	34	5	26	11	9	14	43
Zhen	25	51	3	27	24	42	21	17
Kan	6	40	29	4	7	59	64	47
Gen	33	62	39	52	15	53	56	31
Kun	12	16	8	23	2	20	35	45
Xun	44	32	48	18	46	57	50	28
Li	13	55	63	22	36	37	30	49
Dui	10	54	60	41	19	61	38	58

12

Hexagram 1

Qian

乾

Yang, the active

Work steadily and you will achieve favourable results.

HEXAGRAM 1

First line Yang:
Work on yourself in obscurity.

Second line Yang: Good will come from your undertaking.

Third line Yang: Diligence and alertness protect you from harm.

Fourth line Yang: Follow your inclinations.

Note: The text below is the traditional script explaining the changing lines of the hexagram. The text above is the modern interpretation.

First line Yang: The dragon is submerged. Do not act.

Second line Yang: The dragon is seen in the field. It is worthwhile to see great people.

Third line Yang: Active in the day, alert at night. Even if there is danger, there will be no harm.

Fourth line Yang: One may leap into the deep, but there will be no harm.

HEXAGRAM 1

Fifth line Yang:
Great success is indicated.

Top line Yang:
Things will happen contrary to your wishes. Do not go over the limit.

Using Yang:
There is no limit to what you can achieve.

Fifth line Yang: The dragon is flying in the sky. It is beneficial to see a great person.

Top line Yang: The dragon that flies too high has regrets.

Using Yang: A group of dragons appear with none as leader.

Hexagram 2

Yin, the receptive

Do not force matters but go with the flow.

•

HEXAGRAM 2

First line Yin: Walking on frost, icy conditions approaching.

Second line Yin: When you are honest, straight, and strong, things will work out well without great effort.

Third line Yin: No display of brilliance. Working for a superior, at first he gets nothing but in the end he will have success.

Fourth line Yin: The sack is sealed up. Nothing can go in or come out. No praise or blame.

HEXAGRAM 2

Fifth line Yin: Imperial yellow garment is very auspicious.

Top line Yin: Dragons fight and the blood is dark yellow.

Using Yin: It is favourable to remain steadfast.

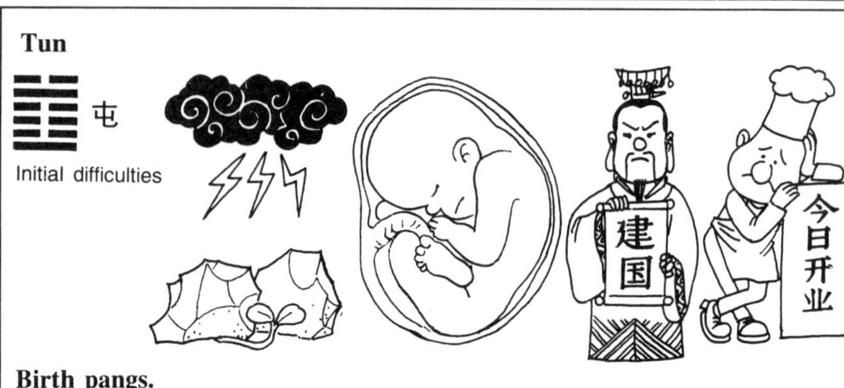

Birth pangs.

First line Yang: Your progress is blocked. Bide your time.

Second line Yin: Unable to advance. Wait for help.

First line Yang: When you are hesitant and not getting anywhere, stay upright. Find helpers.

Second line Yin: Mounted on a horse but at a standstill. A girl is chaste; she declines to marry. She will wed in ten years.

HEXAGRAM 3

Third line Yin: Do not force matters. A no-win situation.

Fourth line Yin: There is hope. Cooperate and press ahead.

Fifth line Yang: Conserve your energy until the time is ripe for action.

Top line Yin: Do not despair but look in other directions.

Third line Yin: Chasing deer without a guide, one only gets lost in the forest. Advancing leads to trouble.

Fourth line Yin: Mounted on a horse but at a standstill. If you seek partnership it bodes well to go ahead. There is no disadvantage.

Fifth line Yang: There is difficulty granting favours to others. It is unfavourable to do things in a big way.

Top line Yin: Mounted on a horse but at a standstill, you weep uncontrollably.

Meng

䷃ 蒙

Immaturity

Recognize your ignorance and educate yourself.

First line Yin: A little justice goes a long way.

Second line Yang: Impose discipline with understanding.

First line Yin: It is advantageous to impose punishment to awaken the ignorant. Letting him advance unrestrained will bring regret.

Second line Yang: It is auspicious to be patient with the ignorant. It is auspicious to marry a woman. The son can run the household.

HEXAGRAM 4

Third line Yin: Do not take a girl to see a rich man, or she will lose herself to no benefit.

Fourth line Yin: It is regrettable to be steeped in ignorance.

Fifth line Yin: Innocence is auspicious.

Top line Yang: Punishing the ignorant child will do no good. It is better to protect him.

HEXAGRAM 5

Be patient and bide your time.

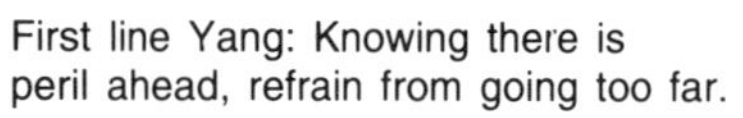
First line Yang: Knowing there is peril ahead, refrain from going too far.

Second line Yang: Difficulty ahead but stay calm to remain unharmed.

First line Yang: He is waiting out in the open country. When there is constancy in virtue, there is no fault.

Second line Yang: Waiting in the mud is precarious.

HEXAGRAM 5

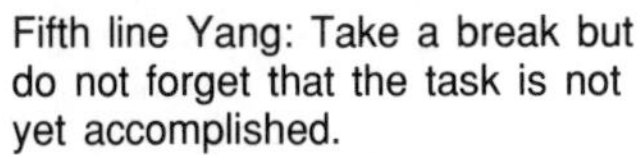

Third line Yang: Waiting in the mud brings on enemies.

Fourth line Yin: Waiting in a place of blood, he must leave the lair.

Fifth line Yang: Waiting with food and wine, perseverance brings good fortune.

Top line Yin: He enters the lair. Three uninvited guests arrive. Treat them properly and all will be well.

Situation of tension.

First line Yin: The way to treat gossip is – in one ear and out the other.

Second line Yang: Make concessions.

First line Yin: If he does not pursue an issue, there may be some talk, but things will go well in the end.

Second line Yang: If he cannot face the challenge, he goes home and hide. In his hometown of three hundred families, there is no trouble.

HEXAGRAM 6

Third line Yin: Though living on past merits, if he remains steadfast he will eventually be lucky. In government work, he will achieve nothing.

Fourth line Yang: His grievance is rejected. Though he suffers loss, it is auspicious for him to stay as he is.

Fifth line Yang: He makes a grievance. Very auspicious.

Top line Yang: He may be presented with a leather belt of honour, but it will be taken away three times in a day.

HEXAGRAM 7

Learn the art of leadership.

First line Yin: When you start something, first be properly organized. Otherwise failure will result.

Strict discipline must be maintained.

First line Yin: An army must set out in an orderly manner. If not, there will be misfortune even if there is a good cause to fight for.

Second line Yang: There is good fortune since the commander is at the centre of the army. He did not put a foot wrong. The king honours him thrice.

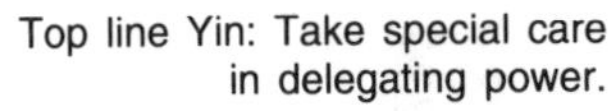

Third line Yin: An army sustains casualties. Misfortune.

Fourth line Yin: An army encamps away from the enemy and avoids harm.

Fifth line Yin: When there are vermin in the fields, getting rid of them is a prudent move. Let the elder son lead the army. If the younger son did, there will be many casualties.

Top line Yin: A great leader selects men to found states and establish powerful houses. He does not pick petty people for the tasks.

HEXAGRAM 8

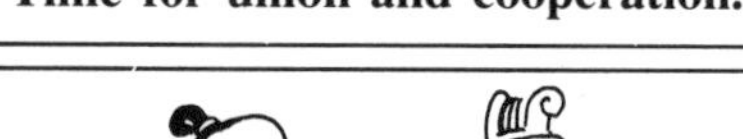
Time for union and cooperation.

First line Yin: Be unaffected in your relationship with others and you will reap unexpected benefits.

First line Yin: Accord with the true is blameless. Truthfulness is like an overflowing plain vessel that brings other good fortune.

Second line Yin: Unity from within oneself bodes well.

HEXAGRAM 8

Third line Yin: Isolated and dejected.

Fourth line Yin: You are in a supportive role. Do it graciously.

Fifth line Yang: Neither regret the past nor have anxiety for the future. Do not force yourself on others.

Top line Yin: The moment for unity has passed. A split is inevitable.

Third line Yin: Alliance with the wrong person.

Fourth line Yin: Unity is sought with those outside his close circle. Auspicious.

Fifth line Yang: The need for unity is evident. The king hunts game on three sides only; he leaves the fourth open as an escape route. When the local people are not wary, it is a good sign.

Top line Yin: Alliance with no leader. Not favourable.

HEXAGRAM 9

From small increments come abundance.

First line Yang: He returns to the true path. Good tidings.

Second line Yang: He is pulled away. Auspicious.

HEXAGRAM 9

Third line Yang: Carriage and axle part. Husband and wife glare at each other.

Fourth line Yin: When there is sincerity, bad blood evaporates and fear dissipates, so there will be no misfortune.

Fifth line Yang: When there is sincerity, he forms a good bond with his neighbours.

Top line Yang: It rains but when the rain stops he can go forward again. It is dangerous to embark on a venture.

Pay close attention to your conduct.

Second line Yang: The person of virtue who withdraws from the mainstream and seeks nothing incurs no trouble.

Rites

Tao

First line Yang: Behaving simply, he encounters no problems.

Second line Yang: Treading a level, easy path, it is auspicious to remain in seclusion.

HEXAGRAM 10

Third line Yin: Able to see with only one eye and able to walk with one leg lame, he steps on a tiger's tail and gets bitten. Misfortune. An army officer behaves in this way for the benefit of his ruler.

Fourth line Yang: Treading on a tiger's tail, be very cautious and it will turn out all right.

Fifth line Yang: He walks resolutely. Although his behaviour is correct, he is surrounded by danger.

Top line Yang: He watches where he treads, he studies the signs. He returns from his journey with supreme good fortune.

HEXAGRAM 11

Tai

☷☰ 泰

Tranquillity

You are on the right path.

First line Yang:
What you do will have
a domino effect to your advantage.

Second line Yang: You have all-round cooperation. No risk.

First line Yang: Pull out a reed and it brings others of its kind with it. A venture will be lucky.

Second line Yang: Crossing the river, he is not swept away. He does not overlook what is far away and does not worry about allies. In this way he accords with balanced action.

Third line Yang: There is no level without an incline, no going without return. Be steadfast and you will not be blamed. Do not worry; your sincerity will help you establish yourself.

Fourth line Yin: He does not rely on his own finances but turns to his neighbours. He puts his confidence in them and does not shun them.

Fifth line Yin: The emperor marries off his younger sister. Good fortune.

Top line Yin: The city wall collapses into the moat. Do not field the army. From the capital comes an order to halt. Going forth will spell trouble.

HEXAGRAM 12

A time of stagnation.

First line Yin: Withdraw from the prevailing turmoil and degeneration and do not get involved.

Second line Yin: Do not fall into the ways of petty people.

First line Yin: Pull out a reed and it brings others of its kind with it. Firm and correct actions bring prosperity.

Second line Yin: The lesser man will be lucky but the obstacles that lie in the great man's path will not deter him from his goal.

HEXAGRAM 12

Third line Yin: It is shameful to be taken in.

Fourth line Yang: When there is order, there is no fault. When his companions come, they rejoice in his blessings.

Fifth line Yang: Obstruction removed, he is happy. He should take care and guard against destruction.

Top line Yang: The blockage is removed. Blocked before, happy afterward.

HEXAGRAM 13

Work hand in hand with others.

First line Yang: Do not be partial as to who you associate with.

Second line Yin: Cliques and exclusivity will lead to narrow-mindedness.

First line Yang: Be like people at the gate and there will be no blame.

Second line Yin: Being like people in a clannish way leads to regret.

HEXAGRAM 13

Third line Yang: Hiding soldiers in the undergrowth and climbing to a hill, he does not take action for three years.

Fourth line Yang: He goes up the city walls but is unable to attack. Good omen.

Fifth line Yang: With others, first cries and then laughter. The great general conquers all in his path.

Top line Yang: One can be like people in the countryside without regret.

HEXAGRAM 14

Da You

大
有

Abundance

Make use of your wealth of experience.

First line Yang: By keeping out of harm's way, you can preserve yourself.

Second line Yang: You have abundant resources and can undertake an important task.

First line Yang: Do not get involved with what is harmful and you will be blameless.

Second line Yang: The great carriage will be safe whichever way it goes.

HEXAGRAM 14

Third line Yang: A duke feasts the Son of Heaven. A little man cannot.

Fourth line Yang: By avoiding ostentation, he averts harm.

Fifth line Yin: The trust that is mutual and imbued with dignity brings favourable results.

Top line Yang: Divine help benefits all.

HEXAGRAM 15

Adapt yourself to circumstances.

First line Yin: Great modesty is the hallmark of the gentleman.

Second line Yin: Modesty that comes from within goes a long way.

First line Yin: With true modesty, the great man is able to cross the river.

Second line Yin: Modesty speaks for itself. Good luck will come from proper conduct.

HEXAGRAM 15

Third line Yang: Do not let fame get into your head but remain humble.

Fourth line Yin: Do not be overwhelmed by flattery and there is no need for a good reputation.

Fifth line Yin: Even modesty can be carried too far. Do not be overmodest.

Top line Yin: Being modest does not mean being weak. Occasionally, a show of strength is appropriate.

Third line Yang: Cultured people who toil yet are humble have good luck in the end.

Fourth line Yin: Maintain modesty always.

Fifth line Yin: He is not considered rich by his neighbour's standards. The time is ripe to make a foray. He does not need wealth to win the goodwill of others.

Top line Yin: His modesty is well-known. It is favourable for him to field an army and march against cities and states.

Harmonize your aims with those of others.

First line Yin: Self-glorification is self-destruction.

Second line Yin: Staying as one is brings good fortune.

First line Yin: He proclaims his happiness. Inauspicious.

Second line Yin: He is rock solid and does not wait until the end of the day.

HEXAGRAM 16

Third line Yin: The sycophant brings more and more suffering upon himself.

Fourth line Yang: Joy comes from within.

Fifth line Yin: Overindulgence in sensual pleasures is like illness tormenting the body.

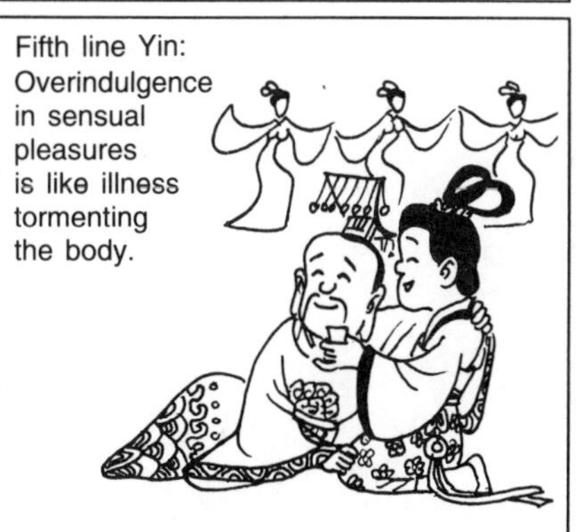

Top line Yin: It is time to be mindful of destructive things or habits and adjust to sober reality.

Third line Yin: If you look up expecting happiness, you will regret it. Delay results in sorrow.

Fourth line Yang: Being a source of joy, there is great gain. Friends will gather around you.

Fifth line Yin: He is steadfast and although ailing does not die.

Top line Yin: Happiness at a climax. If he has the strength to change direction, there will be no fault.

HEXAGRAM 17

Lie low and be of service to others.

First line Yang: Keep pace with the people's wishes.

Second line Yin: Nearby friends or neighbours are preferable to distant relatives.

First line Yang: The official changes. He is fortunate because of his wise behaviour. Relationships outside the gate have merit.

Second line Yin: He gets involved with a child and loses an adult.

HEXAGRAM 17

Third line Yin: An ignoble existence is dragged out just for the sake of staying alive.

Fourth line Yang: Do not sacrifice virtue for gain.

Fifth line Yang: He who heeds the advice of subordinates can achieve much.

Top line Yin: Someone has a hold over you, and you have to work with him whether you like it or not.

Third line Yin: Getting involved with an adult, he loses a child.

Fourth line Yang: He follows the adult and rejects the child. By following such a course he will find what he is looking for. He will benefit by staying on the right path.

Fifth line Yang: Faithfulness is rewarded. Good fortune.

Top line Yin: If you have ties with something, you share its fate. The king offers sacrifices.

HEXAGRAM 18

Gu

Act decisively to put things right.

First line Yin: Make the best of a messy situation.

Second line Yang: Avoid excess in favour of moderation.

First line Yin: The son clears up the mess caused by his father. If he is diligent, everything will work out well in the end.

Second line Yang: In sorting out the mess caused by the mother, the son should not be overzealous.

HEXAGRAM 18

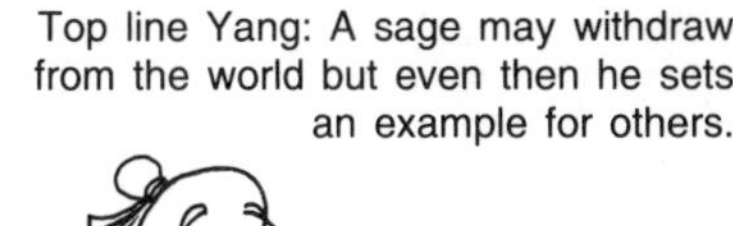

Third line Yang: The son sorts out the mess caused by his father. There is little regret and no great blame.

Fourth line Yin: He tolerates the mess caused by his father; if he continues like this he will be humiliated.

Fifth line Yin: The son clears up the mess caused by his father and wins praise.

Top line Yang: He does not want to work for kings or lords since he has set his sights on something higher.

Make good use of your advantageous position.

First line Yang: He oversees things in a sensitive manner. Auspicious.

Second line Yang: Overseeing things in a sensitive manner will not fail to benefit others.

HEXAGRAM 19

Third line Yin: Improper overseeing brings no benefit. He who looks before he leaps will not make any mistakes.

Fourth line Yin: Perfect overseeing is blameless.

Fifth line Yin: Knowlegeable overseeing is the mark of a good leader. Auspicious.

Top line Yin: Attentive overseeing is impeccable.

Time for stocktaking. Take a good look at yourself.

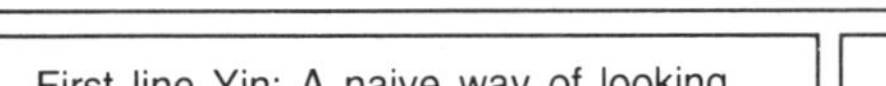

First line Yin: A naive way of looking at things.

Second line Yin: Seeing things from a limited viewpoint, your conclusions are limited and subjective.

First line Yin: He sees things in a childish way. This is all right for lesser men but not the superior man.

Second line Yin: Peeking out from within, passive like a woman.

HEXAGRAM 20

Third line Yin: He examines his life so that he can decide whether to advance or retreat.

Fourth line Yin: It is useful to be the king's guest in order to find out about the state's achievements.

Fifth line Yang: He examines his own life. The wise man does no wrong.

Top line Yang: He examines the life of others. He will not lapse into error.

HEXAGRAM 21

First line Yang: He wears fetters on his feet. This averts harm.

Second line Yin: He bites into flesh so deeply that it covers his nose. No blame.

HEXAGRAM 21

Third line Yin: He bites into dried meat and is poisoned. A little trouble but no harm.

Fourth line Yang: He bites into dried meat and finds a bronze arrowhead. It is favourable to persevere in the face of adversity. Good fortune.

Fifth line Yin: Biting into dried meat, he finds a small piece of gold. If steadfast amid danger, there will be no trouble.

Top line Yang: He wears a cangue that covers his ears. There will be ill fortune.

HEXAGRAM 22

Package things well.

First line Yang: His feet are adorned. He leaves his carriage and walks.

Second line Yin: He adorns his beard.

HEXAGRAM 22

Third line Yang: Do not emphasize form over substance.

Fourth line Yin: The plain but virtuous is preferable to the glamorous but degenerate.

Fifth line Yin: Inner feelings and sincerity count, not the finery and show of wealth.

Top line Yang: Renounce artifice and return to simplicity.

Third line Yang: Adorned and dazzling, he is lucky if he remains steadfast and true.

Fourth line Yin: Adorned yet plain, a white horse is fleet-footed.

Fifth line Yin: Though adorned like a hill garden, the bolts of cloth he offers are few. His difficulties will end in good fortune.

Top line Yang: Plain adornment is impeccable. Harm averted.

Put things on hold.

First line Yin: A tiny hole can cause the collapse of a great dyke.

Second line Yin: Things go from bad to worse.

First line Yin: He breaks the leg of the bed. It is bad to destroy anything that is good.

Second line Yin: He breaks the frame of the bed. It is bad to destroy anything that is useful.

HEXAGRAM 23

Third line Yin: Maintain your integrity and there will be no friction.

Fourth line Yin: You are on the edge of disaster. Endure the inevitable and look ahead to rebuilding.

Fifth line Yin: Mutual help. Cooperation in living.

Top line Yang: Total collapse. Utter failure.

Third line Yin: He is the one who breaks things. This is not a mistake.

Fourth line Yin: He breaks both the bed and the bedcover. This is bad.

Fifth line Yin: A fish on a string but cherished like a palace lady. Not unfavourable.

Top line Yang: The biggest fruit is not eaten. The lord gains chariots, the little man has his hut destroyed.

HEXAGRAM 24

Fu

A time for renewal.

First line Yang: He acknowledges his mistakes and returns to goodness.

Second line Yin: It is a blessing to correct oneself in the nick of time.

First line Yang: He returns before going far. There will be no regret. He will be very fortunate.

Second line Yin: Fine return. Auspicious.

HEXAGRAM 24

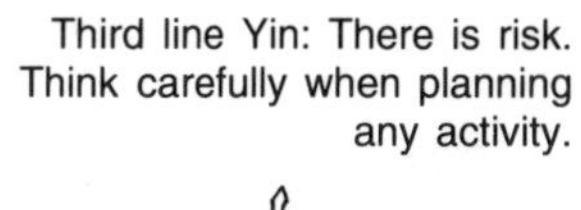

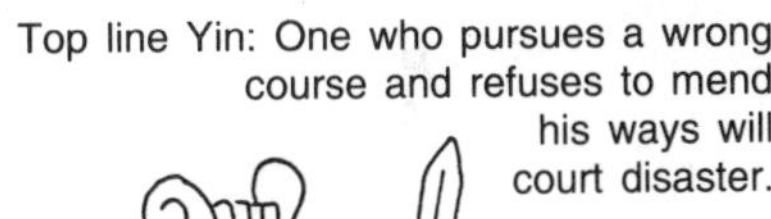

Third line Yin: He returns many times. Danger but no harm.

Fourth line Yin: He starts out with others but returns alone.

Fifth line Yin: He returns with dignity. There is no regret.

Top line Yin: He has been given misleading information about his return. This is bad. There will be disaster. If he calls for a military expedition, there will be a resounding defeat, boding ill for the leader of the nation. Even in ten years there will be no victory.

Be spontaneous and act without hope of personal gain.

First line Yang:
Trust your own heart. Fortune smiles on the pure and innocent.

Second line Yin: You should do the things that you can do well.

First line Yang: He advances without deviation. Auspicious.

Second line Yin: If he has not ploughed for the harvest and has not prepared new fields, then it is profitable to have somewhere to go.

HEXAGRAM 25

Third line Yin: He who does not know his limitations courts disaster.

Fourth line Yang: If you stand firm, all will be well.

Fifth line Yang: If you encounter a problem that is not caused by you, ride it out rather then grapple with it. Let it run its course and the matter will fix itself.

Top line Yang: If you do not think things through carefully but try to push ahead stubbornly, you run the risk of disaster.

Third line Yin: Unexpected misfortune. Though the ox was tethered, it becomes the traveller's gain and the villager's loss.

Fourth line Yang: If he is able to be true to himself, there will be no mistakes.

Fifth line Yang: Unexpected illness. He is cured without taking medicine.

Top line Yang: He is not wrong, yet if he tries to move he will be in difficulties.

HEXAGRAM 26

Da Chu

大
畜

The taming power of the great

A time of potential. Act prudently.

First line Yang: Conserve your resources and wait for an appropriate time to act.

Second line Yang: You fail to make headway. Conserve your energy for a greater effort.

First line Yang: There is danger. It is wise to halt.

Second line Yang: The carriage has its axles removed.

HEXAGRAM 26

Third line Yang: Harness your talents and do not be impulsive.

Fourth line Yin: Show restraint and do not take unnecessary risks.

Fifth line Yin: Deal with the source of problems and not the symptoms.

Top line Yang: All obstacles have been removed. You can put your stored energy to unlimited use. A notable success is possible.

Third line Yang: Fine horses surge forward. It is favourable to persevere. A well-drilled chariot stands guard. It is favourable to advance.

Fourth line Yin: The young bull is restrained by a horn guard. There will be good fortune.

Fifth line Yin: The gelded boar does not use its tusks. Auspicious.

Top line Yang: He is on heaven's road. Blessed state.

First line Yang: It is bad luck to ignore your sacred tortoise and watch me with your jaw dropping.

Second line Yin: He turns everything upside down for nourishment. It goes against the tradition of seeking nourishment above the ground. This will lead to evil.

HEXAGRAM 27

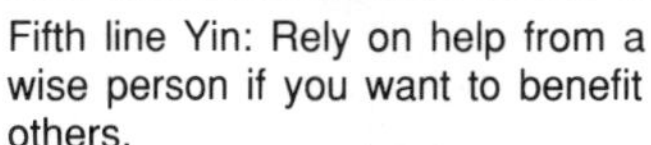

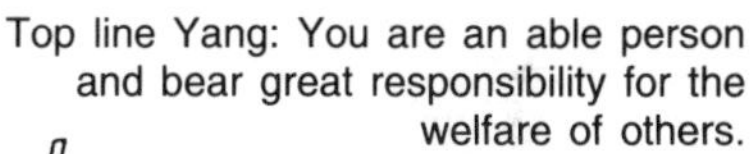

Third line Yin: He rejects nourishment. This will be bad, no matter how firm he is. He does nothing for ten years. Unfavourable.

Fourth line Yin: Reverse nourishment is lucky. A tiger gazing down, about to give chase, is not blamed.

Fifth line Yin: In abnormal situations, he will be lucky if he remains steadfast and true. He must not try to ford a great river.

Top line Yang: To be a source of nourishment is dangerous yet auspicious. It is favourable to ford a great river.

Things are strained to the breaking point.

First line Yin: Pay attention to all the details before you begin anything.

First line Yin: He uses white woven mats to place offerings. Blameless.

Second line Yang: The ageing willow sprouts new shoots. The old man takes a young wife. Favourable.

HEXAGRAM 28

Third line Yang: The main support is weak. This is bad.

Fourth line Yang: The main support has held. This is auspicious. Otherwise it would have been embarrassing.

Fifth line Yang: The ageing willow bears flowers. The old woman marries a young man. No blame and no praise. The flowers of an old tree are without fragrance. The marriage of an old woman will not produce children.

Top line Yin: He crosses the river and the water rises above his head. It is inauspicious but there is no harm.

HEXAGRAM 29

Roll with the flow to ride out danger.

First line Yin: Be careful not to lose your way in what you do.

Second line Yang: Although you are in a dangerous situation, try to keep your head above water.

First line Yin: He gets into a whirlpool. Misfortune. He does not examine the flow of water and recklessly tries to ford the river.

Second line Yang: Surging waters all around him. He needs to be prudent.

HEXAGRAM 29

Third line Yin: He is confronted by the watery depths, whether he advances or retreats. He should stop and rest, otherwise he will sink.

Fourth line Yin: A jug of wine, a bowl of grain, and extra jars of each are passed in by a rope through the watery depths. In the end, he comes to no harm.

Fifth line Yang: The watery depths are not overflowing. Order is approaching. No risk.

Top line Yin: He is tied up with ropes and imprisoned behind walls of thorn bushes. For three years he cannot escape. Misfortune.

HEXAGRAM 30

Coöperate willingly. Dependence.

First line Yang: When his steps are awry and he is heedful of this, there will be no mistakes.

Second line Yin: Yellow light. Supremely auspicious.

HEXAGRAM 30

Third line Yang: He who does not bestir himself in his youth will have cause for regret in his old age.

Fourth line Yang: You are too impatient and restless. You will exhaust yourself because of your avarice.

Fifth line Yin: The good leader shows concern for others before himself, and enjoys himself only after everyone else finds enjoyment.

Top line Yang: Do not be extreme in eradicating anything. Do not judge others too harshly.

Third line Yang: In the light of the setting sun, he drums on a pot or sighs the lament of the elderly, which is unfortunate.

Fourth line Yang: Reckless action results in burnout, death, and abandonment.

Fifth line Yin: He weeps and bemoans. Auspicious.

Top line Yang: The king uses him for attack. He kills the leaders but spares the followers. He is not blamed.

HEXAGRAM 31

Welcome those who approach.

First line Yin: The start of mutual attraction. Do not go overboard.

Second line Yin: Do not get carried away by sudden impulses.

First line Yin: He moves his toes.

Second line Yin: He moves his calves. Inauspicious. He should stay where he is.

HEXAGRAM 31

Third line Yang: He moves his thighs. But someone grabs his heels. Advancing will lead to trouble.

Fourth line Yang: Keeping on brings good fortune. Regrets will pass. Friends around him accord with his wishes.

Fifth line Yang: He moves his back. No regrets.

Top line Yin: He moves his cheeks and his tongue.

HEXAGRAM 32

First line Yin: It is the beginning of a relationship and there are excessive demands.

Second line Yang: Self-restraint leads to mutual respect and appreciation.

First line Yin: To be overpersistent will result in unhappy consequences. Unfavourable.

Second line Yang: Regret passes.

HEXAGRAM 32

Third line Yang: He does not persist in virtue and suffers disgrace.

Fourth line Yang: There is no game in the field.

Fifth line Yin: He keeps to his station. Auspicious for a wife, inauspicious for a husband.

Top line Yin: He constantly exerts himself. Misfortune.

Make a strategic withdrawal.

First line Yin: He fixes his gaze upwards only and is in danger of losing his balance.

Second line Yin: The more you try to retain someone, the more determined he is to leave.

First line Yin: Danger at the tail end of a withdrawal. Do not move further.

Second line Yin: He grasps tightly and will not let go.

HEXAGRAM 33

Third line Yang:
Beware of getting involved for selfish gains.

Fourth line Yang:
The wise person knows how to make a timely withdrawal and avoid being harmed.

Fifth line Yang: He knows when to advance and when to retreat.
He is victorious and not defeated.

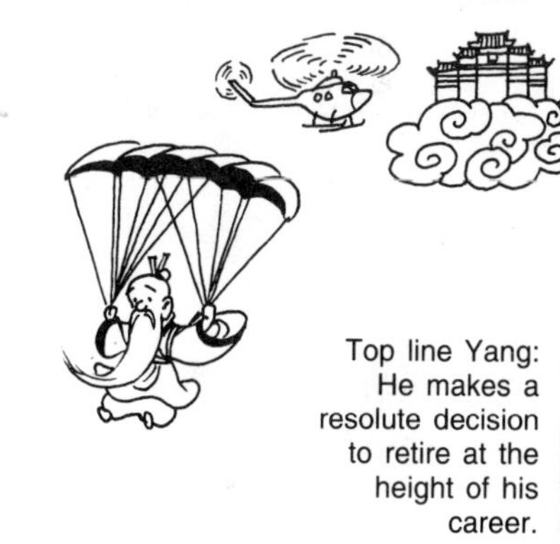

Top line Yang:
He makes a resolute decision to retire at the height of his career.

Third line Yang: He withdraws but there are problems and dangers. Taking care of helpers or concubines is auspicious.

Fourth line Yang: Wise people who withdraw in the right way are fortunate; petty people are not.

Fifth line Yang: He hides himself away very carefully. Correct behaviour bodes well.

Top line Yang: When the person of means withdraws serenely, others benefit.

HEXAGRAM 34

Da Zhuang

大
壮

Power of the great

Use your strength prudently.

First line Yang: He is arrogant and flaunts his power, but will suffer a setback.

Second line Yang: He is strong and upright, but does not flaunt his strength.

First line Yang: His strength lies in his toes. Marching forth leads to misfortune.

Second line Yang: He will be fortunate if he remains upright and true.

HEXAGRAM 34

Third line Yang: Petty people use force while the wise do not. To be unbending is dangerous. Use your wit, not your fist; for if you use force, you will be like a ram butting a fence and getting its horns caught instead.

Fourth line Yang: Correct behaviour will bring good fortune and regrets pass away. He overcomes obstacles through his strength, which is like the hubs of a great carriage.

Fifth line Yin: He abandons his ram-like nature. No regret.

Top line Yin: The ram butts a fence. He cannot pull back and cannot go on. He cannot continue like this. If he understands the danger, there will be good fortune.

A time to make progress.

First line Yin: Do not resist or react. Just be natural and go along with things.

Second line Yin: Your progress is halted. Persevere with a sense of duty.

First line Yin: He advances and comes under strain. If he behaves properly, all will work out well. To slacken his advance and be faithful to his ruler will avert harm.

Second line Yin: He advances sorrowfully. If he behaves properly he will receive blessings from his heavenly mother.

HEXAGRAM 35

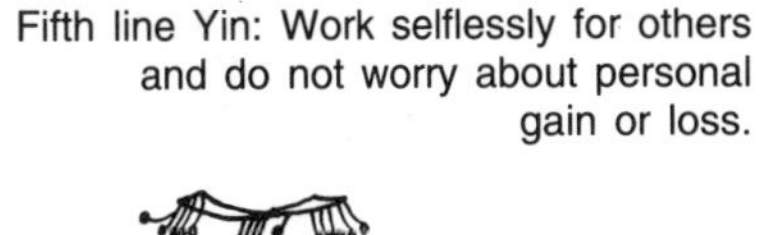

Third line Yin: Everyone trusts him and regret vanishes.

Fourth line Yang: He advances like a rat. It is dangerous for him to go on.

Fifth line Yin: All regrets have now gone. Do not worry about loss or gain. To advance is favourable and brings many advantages.

Top line Yang: Like a ram advancing its horns, he uses his strengths for aggression. It is dangerous to do so, but there is no harm in the end.

First line Yang: The brightness is dimmed with flying and he lowers his wings. Wise people on a journey do not eat for three days. Going somewhere, the subject is criticized by the ruler.

Second line Yin: Brightness is dimmed. He is injured in the left thigh. If his horse is strong, he will be rescued and there will be good fortune.

HEXAGRAM 36

Fifth line Yin: Maintain your integrity in spite of difficulty. Adopt a humble position if you have to.

Third Yang line: Brightness is dimmed and he goes hunting in the south. Even if the big chieftains are caught, order cannot be restored quickly.

Fourth Yin line: He enters the left side of the belly. He reaches the heart of that which dims the brightness. He leaves through the courtyard gate.

Fifth Yin line: Wherever brightness is dimmed, be like the scion of a royal house. It is beneficial to be upright and true.

Top line Yin: Not bright but dark. First he flies up to the sky. Then he goes underground.

HEXAGRAM 37

Jia Ren

Find your place in the scheme of things.

First line Yang: Spell out the rules clearly to prevent wrongdoing.

Second line Yin: Sharing of work is fair. Each one has his or her part to play.

First line Yang: He has rules in the family. Regrets vanish.

Second line Yin: She does not go outside and follow her desires. She stays inside the home preparing meals. It is auspicious for her to continue.

HEXAGRAM 37

Third line Yang: Find a delicate balance between discipline and severity.

Fourth line Yin: Harmony is prosperity.

Fifth line Yang: When there is harmony and love, the family is blessed indeed.

Top line Yang: Set a good example and others will learn from you.

Third line Yang: The household complains of excessive severity. Regretting it will turn danger into good fortune. If the women and children are frivolous, there will be trouble.

Fourth line Yin: A prosperous house. Extremely good fortune.

Fifth line Yang: The king is very forgiving with his family. There is nothing to worry about. Auspicious.

Top line Yang: His regal presence fills them with awe. Good fortune in the end.

HEXAGRAM 38

A time of estrangement and opposition.

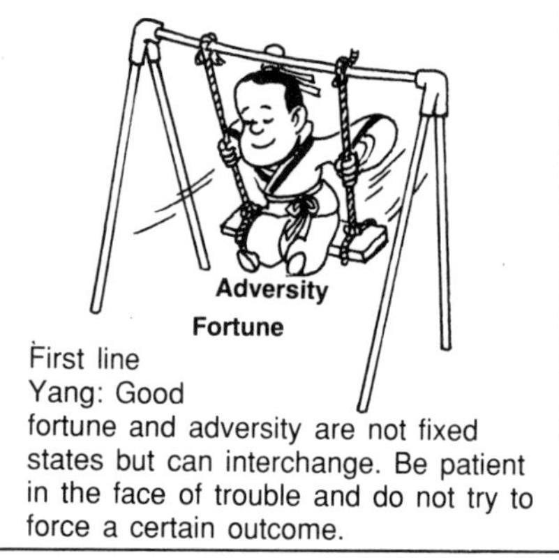

First line Yang: Good fortune and adversity are not fixed states but can interchange. Be patient in the face of trouble and do not try to force a certain outcome.

Second line Yang: Do not fear obstacles ahead and you will have meaningful encounters.

First line Yang: Regrets will pass. Do not chase the runaway horse. It will come back on its own. It will see someone horrible and return. No harm.

Second line Yang: By chance he meets his master in an alley. No harm.

HEXAGRAM 38

Third line Yin: After a long separation comes a reunion. Things will turn out all right in the end.

Fourth line Yang: You may feel isolated from others. But cooperation with a wise man will benefit both.

Fifth line Yin: You will meet a trustworthy person and it is good to cooperate.

Top line Yang: Deal calmly with any fears that are troubling you. A quiet, calm approach will clear away your anxieties just as the sky clears after a rainstorm.

Third line Yin: Having the carriage dragged and the ox halted, that person is being punished by heaven. This is not a good start, but the end will be better.

Fourth line Yang: Estranged and alone, he meets a great man. He gives his allegiance and danger passes without harm to him.

Fifth line Yin: Regrets will pass. When the clan has punished its own, what is wrong with proceeding onward?

Top line Yang: Estranged and alone, he sees the pig covered with filth and a carriage full of demons. At first the bow is drawn, then it is put down. He does not seek plunder but marriage. Going forward, he encounters rain and this is auspicious.

You must overcome an obstacle ahead.

First line Yin: Danger ahead. Pause and wait patiently for the right moment to act instead of blindly blundering on.

First line Yin: The way ahead is blocked. Returning will bring praise.

Second line Yin: The servant of a king faces many difficulties. He is not to be blamed.

HEXAGRAM 39

Third line Yang:
Do not endanger yourself needlessly but retreat to preserve yourself.

Fourth line Yin: He gets help to deal with the problem.

Fifth line Yang: You can count on the help of others when there is trouble.

Top line Yin: With the help of strong allies, the menace is subdued.

Third line Yang: He goes forward and encounters obstruction. So he turns around and comes back.

Fourth line Yin: To go forward is to encounter obstruction. By returning he is united.

Fifth line Yang: The obstruction is great. His friends rally around him.

Top line Yin: Going forward is to face obstacle. It is better to turn back. It is worthwhile seeing great people.

Your luck will change for the better.

Second line Yang: He is not proud or lazy. It is auspicious for him to take on responsibilities.

First line Yin: Going forward, it is auspicious to go early. No harm.

Second line Yang: He catches three foxes on a hunt. He receives a golden arrow. To be upright brings good fortune.

HEXAGRAM 40

Third line Yin:
The person of means who is conceited will meet with calamity.

Fourth line Yang: He rids himself of bad habits and wins the trust and confidence of friends.

Fifth line Yin: It is prudent to keep aloof. Watch out for flatterers and false friends.

Top line Yin: The situation is not hopeless. Aim high and act forcefully, and you will succeed.

Third line Yin: The burdened man travels in a carriage and this attracts robbers who attack him. Keeping on will lead to trouble.

Fourth line Yang: He gets a toe free. Friends come and put their faith in him.

Fifth line Yin: The wise man sets himself free. Auspicious. This makes lesser men have faith in him.

Top line Yin: The lord shoots an arrow at a hawk perched on a wall and hits it. Advantageous move.

Sun

损

Decrease

A period of decrease.

First line Yang: Complete your own work but at the same time show your generosity by helping others. Spread your bounty.

Second line Yang: When there is something good, do not ask for more or for less.

First line Yang: He leaves his own work and goes to help another person. There is no regret if he weighs the matter carefully.

Second line Yang: It is good to be upright, but it would be unlucky to go on a venture. He who helps others will inevitably help himself.

HEXAGRAM 41

Third line Yin: Three men travel together, but one disagrees with the others and leaves. He then finds another person as a companion.

Fourth line Yin: Reducing fever hastens the joy of recovery. Harm averted.

Fifth line Yin: If given ten tortoise shells, no one is able to refuse. Supreme good fortune.

Top line Yang: Not reduction but increase. No harm. It is good to stay upright. It is favourable to advance. You attract able helpers, not just relatives.

A period of increase.

First line Yang: You have the energy to undertake some great work. Stay humble and selfless, and you will be very fortunate.

Second line Yin: He gets along well with those above and below him, and there is benefit and no harm.

First line Yang: It is favourable to do great deeds. Supreme good fortune. No harm.

Second line Yin: If given ten tortoise shells, no one can refuse. He will be fortunate as long as he behaves properly. The king makes offerings to the Lord of Heaven. Auspicious.

HEXAGRAM 42

Third line Yin: He gains by inauspicious actions and comes to no harm. He walks the straight path and, using the seal of authority, announces himself to the prince.

Fourth line Yin: He walks the true path. He announces himself to the prince who will follow. It is good to be relied upon, even to the extent of helping to shift the capital.

Fifth line Yang: There is faithfulness in his heart. Not to seek is supreme good fortune. Virtue comes naturally.

Top line Yang: Do not increase something so much that it might be attacked. Do not be so insistent about things that it leads to trouble.

First line Yang: He steps forward boldly. Advance brings no victory but harm.

Second line Yang: When wary and alert, even if there are attackers in the night, there is no worry.

HEXAGRAM 43

Third line Yang: He puts his face upfront and this brings misfortune. The wise man walks alone and encounters rain. He gets wet. He is annoyed but there is no regret.

Fourth line Yang: The skin on his buttocks is stripped away and he walks with difficulty. If he were led like a sheep, it would be all right. One may hear words without believing.

Fifth line Yang: Pleasant yet decisive, balanced behaviour is blameless.

Top line Yin: There is no cry of warning; misfortune in the end.

HEXAGRAM 44

Gou

姤

Contact

Beware of temptation.

First line Yin: His desire is aroused and he cannot resist the temptation.

Second line Yang: But his rival wins the woman's affection first.

First line Yin: He should be restrained with an iron brake. It bodes well to be upright. If he goes forward, he will encounter misfortune. He is like an emaciated pig who rushes around.

Second line Yang: When the fish is in the bag, there is no problem but it does not benefit a guest.

Fourth line Yang: He resorts to force and trouble is inevitable.

Third line Yang: The skin on his buttocks has been stripped away and he has difficulty walking. There is danger but no harm.

Fourth line Yang: No fish in the bag. There will be misfortune.

Fifth line Yang: Wrapping a melon with willow leaves is like trying to conceal one's brilliance. It comes as though from heaven.

Top line Yang: As though attacked by the horns of some wild animal, he meets up with trouble by accident. There will be trouble but no great harm.

HEXAGRAM 45

A time to form strong bonds.

First line Yin: If there is no common aim, there will be chaos.

Second line Yin: There is sincerity and goodwill. Cooperation instead of antagonism.

First line Yin: Their faithfulness is not complete: sometimes they are disorderly, sometimes they are together. If they obeyed the call, they would be smiling. Do not worry. Go forward and there will be no harm.

Second line Yin: He is led forward and there is good fortune. No harm. As long as he is sincere, even the smallest offering will be beneficial.

Third line Yin: There is loss but this is compensated by some other gain.

Fourth line Yang: He devotes himself to meeting the aspirations of the people and carries out his work in a responsible manner.

Fifth line Yang: Although he holds a high position, his actions accord with the people's wishes.

Top line Yin: He gets rebuffed and is dejected.

Third line Yin: Gathering around a leader, they lament. Unfavourable. Going forward brings no harm, just a little trouble.

Fourth line Yang: Great fortune. No blame.

Fifth line Yang: When they are gathered around the man of rank, no one blames the insincere. If the basis is always true, regret disappears.

Top line Yin: He sighs and wails. No blame.

HEXAGRAM 46

A favourable time to advance by degrees.

First line Yin: Like the blooming of plants in spring, a scene of thriving prosperity.

Second line Yang: Proceed systematically.

First line Yin: He rises and is trusted. Great good fortune.

Second line Yang: If he is sincere, even the smallest offerings will be beneficial. No harm.

HEXAGRAM 46

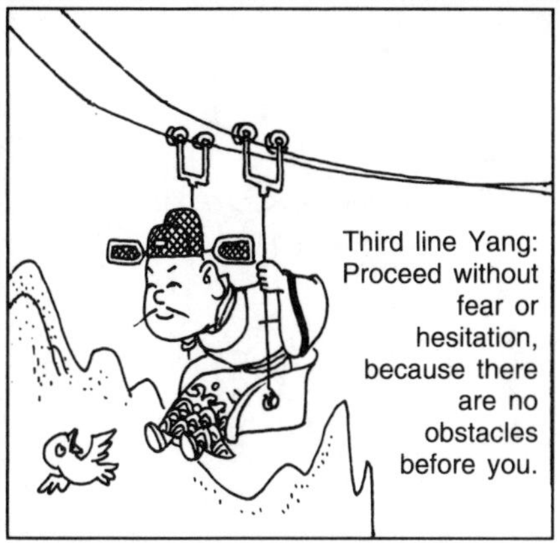

Third line Yang: He rises in an empty realm.

Fourth line Yin: The king makes offerings on a mountain. Auspicious. No harm.

Fifth line Yin: He behaves properly and is fortunate. He ascends the steps.

Top line Yin: Rising from obscurity benefits from unending steadfastness.

HEXAGRAM 47

Meet adversity with resolution.

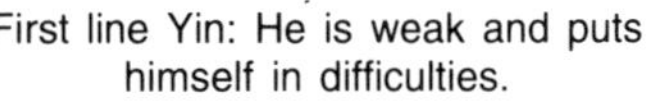
First line Yin: He is weak and puts himself in difficulties.

Second line Yang: He gets out of difficulty and has become optimistic.

First line Yin: He is sitting exhausted on a tree stump. He wanders into a dark valley. For three years he is not seen.

Second line Yang: Exhausted of food and drink. The red apron of high office is awarded to him. He should make offerings. Moving forward brings bad fortune, but there is no great mistake.

Third line Yin: Weighed down by boulders, he leans for support on thorns. He enters his palace but his wife is not there. Misfortune.

Fourth line Yang: He moves slowly, bogged down in a bronze carriage. But his difficulties will have an end.

Fifth line Yang: His nose and feet are cut off. The red robe of high office is a burden to him. Slowly, he gets free. It is worthwhile to make offerings.

Top line Yin: Held by tangled vines and in distress, he will not regret moving. It bodes well to go forth.

Second line Yang: It is too early for an undertaking. Your efforts will be wasted.

First line Yin: The well is muddy. No one drinks. No creatures come to an old well.

Second line Yang: The depths of the well provide enough for a minnow. The broken jar leaks.

HEXAGRAM 48

Third line Yang: The well is clear, but no one drinks. It is a pain to one's heart. It can be drawn upon, and when the ruler understands, all will receive its blessings.

Fourth line Yin: The well is well-lined. There will be no problems.

Fifth line Yang: The well is pure. People drink from its cool spring.

Top line Yin: He draws from the well without difficulty, because it is not covered. Truthfulness is very auspicious.

HEXAGRAM 49

Accept revolutionary changes.

First line Yang: Inadequate preparation, so do not rush into action.

Second line Yin: The time is ripe; take action immediately.

First line Yang: For strength, use yellow cowhide.

Second line Yin: When the time comes, he is able to make changes. Initiating action is most favourable. There will be no harm.

HEXAGRAM 49

Fifth line Yang: The time has come for revolutionary changes and he achieves remarkable success.

Third line Yang: Going forth is dangerous. If he wishes to change things, he will need to speak about it three times, then people will have faith in it.

Fourth line Yang: Regret vanishes. Allegiance is shown to him. It is favourable to make revolutionary changes.

Fifth line Yang: The great man changes like a tiger. Even though he has not consulted the oracle, people have confidence in him.

Top line Yin: The great man changes like a leopard, whereas the lesser man simply changes his facial appearance. To advance will bring bad fortune. To maintain one's integrity is auspicious.

Ding

鼎

The cauldron

Lay the groundwork for something new.

First line Yin: Overturning a cauldron makes cleaning easier. In the same way, remove bad habits before you embark on any venture.

Second line Yang: Do not leave yourself open to criticism. Keep on improving things.

First line Yin: When the cauldron is overturned, it is easier to remove anything bad. When one takes a concubine, as long as she bears a son there is no blame.

Second line Yang: The cauldron is filled with food. My antagonists are jealous but they cannot harm me. Auspicious.

HEXAGRAM 50

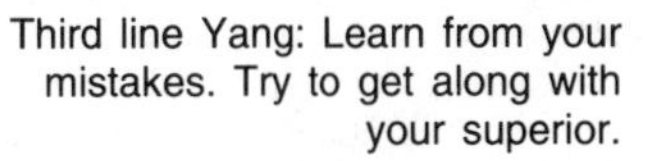

Third line Yang: Learn from your mistakes. Try to get along with your superior.

Fourth line Yang: Carelessness and incompetence result in failure.

Fifth line Yin: Strengthen your good qualities.

Top line Yang: The wise and good person benefits all those fortunate enough to come into contact with him.

Third line Yang: The handles of the cauldron have been changed. They cannot be used. The fat pheasant's meat in it is uneaten. Just when it rains, regret diminishes, and there is good fortune in the end.

Fourth line Yang: The cauldron's legs break and the duke's food is spilled. There will be severe punishment. Misfortune.

Fifth line Yin: The cauldron's handles and carrying rod are made of golden bronze. It is helpful to remain upright.

Top line Yang: The cauldron's carrying rod is made of jade. Very good fortune and everything works to his advantage.

A blessing in disguise. Awakening jolt.

First line Yang: The crack of a thunderbolt strikes terror. But there is mirthful talk afterwards. Auspicious.

Second line Yin: Thunderbolts. Danger. He loses his treasures and flees to the high hills. He must not go after them. In seven days he will get them back.

HEXAGRAM 51

Third line Yin: Terrified beyond description, he is at his wit's end. He needs to have the presence of mind to stay calm.

Fourth line Yang: He is shocked into immobility by some unexpected calamity. He must snap out of it.

Fifth line Yin: He is aware of danger and knows how to weather the storm.

Top line Yin: Danger is imminent. Take to your heels to stay out of harm.

Third line Yin: Thunderbolts boom, shocking him into taking flight. There is nothing wrong with this.

Fourth line Yang: The thunderbolt hits the mud.

Fifth line Yin: There are thunderbolts but there is no problem because he has things to attend to.

Top line Yin: Thunderbolts make him tremble and he stares at them anxiously. Initiating action will bring bad fortune. When thunder does not affect the individual but does affect the neighbourhood, there is no blame. If a partnership is formed, there is talk.

HEXAGRAM 52

Gen

艮

Keeping still

A time to quieten your heart.

First line Yin: When things are stopped at the outset, matters never reach the point of losing what is right, so there is no fault.

Second line Yin: Steadfast and unmoved by temptation.

First line Yin: There is nothing wrong with resting his toes. It is favourable for him to be virtuous always.

Second line Yin: He rests his legs. He is unable to save the person whom he follows and is uneasy in his heart.

HEXAGRAM 52

Third line Yang: He rests his loins, and his back is laid open. There is danger and his heart burns with anxiety.

Fourth line Yin: He rests his body. There is no blame.

Fifth line Yin: He rests his jaws. His speech is proper. There will be no regrets.

Top line Yang: He rests with care. There will be good fortune.

First line Yin: Take life step by step and you will not run into danger.

Second line Yin: Build up your strength and advance at the appropriate time.

First line Yin: As geese gradually make their way onto shore, if the little ones struggle, advice is handed out, not blame.

Second line Yin: The geese make their way to a boulder and eat and drink happily there. There will be good fortune.

HEXAGRAM 53

Third line Yang: The geese make their way across the land. A husband marches to war and does not return. A wife becomes pregnant but does not give birth. Misfortune. It is favourable to repel attacks, not make them.

Fourth line Yin: The geese gradually go up a tree and roost on a level surface. There will be no mistakes.

Fifth line Yang: The geese gradually approach the mountain. This is like a wife who does not become pregnant for three years. In the end she conceives, as nothing can prevent this. There will be good fortune.

Top line Yang: The wild geese gradually soar to the heights. Their feathers can be used for ritual dances. There will be good fortune.

Gui Mei

归妹

Marriageable maiden

Know your proper place.

First line Yang: Your position is low but you exercise tact, modesty, and kindness.

Second line Yang: Do not lose heart but persevere, whatever the circumstances.

First line Yang: The maiden marries as a concubine. This is like a lame man who manages to get along. It is auspicious for her to advance.

Second line Yang: She sees dimly. It is favourable for her to remain in seclusion.

HEXAGRAM 54

Third line Yin: A maiden going to marry does so with expectations; instead she marries as a concubine.

Fourth line Yang: The maiden's marriage is delayed. A late marriage comes in its time.

Fifth line Yin: When the emperor marries off his younger sister, her clothes are not as gorgeous as those of her attendants. The moon is almost full. Supremely auspicious.

Top line Yin: The bride receives a chest that is empty. The groom sacrifices a sheep but there is no blood. Unfavourable.

HEXAGRAM 55

Things are at a peak or climax.

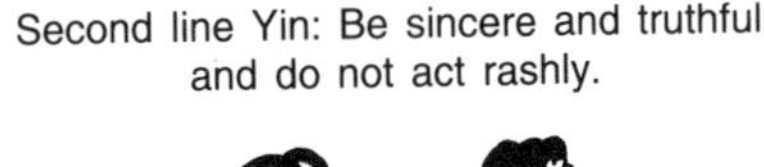

First line Yang: He meets his supreme leader. There is nothing wrong in the fact that they are alike. It will be praiseworthy to go forth.

Second line Yin: Abundance is as a canopy on which you see the Pole Star in the daytime. Going forward, you will be met with suspicion and disdain. It is auspicious if you are truthful in an evident way.

HEXAGRAM 55

Third line Yang: Overindulgence leads to self-destruction.

Fourth line Yang: Advice from the right person is beneficial to you.

Fifth line Yin: If you work with reliable and honest companions, you will have nothing to worry about.

Top line Yin: You are arrogant and ambitious and will achieve the opposite of what you are striving for.

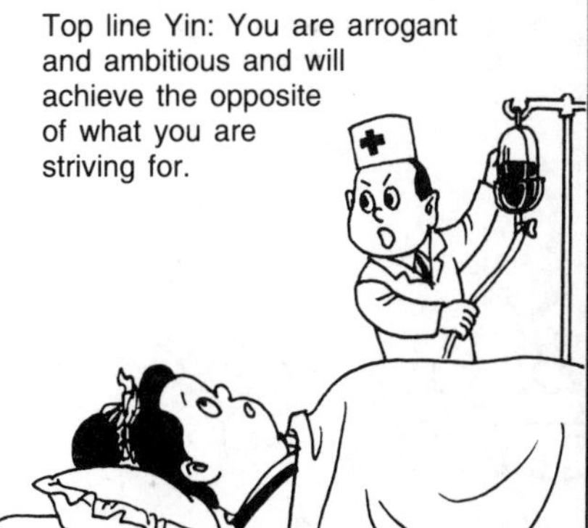

Third line Yang: His abundance is like a banner through which he can see the stars at midday. He breaks his arm but there will be no blame.

Fourth line Yang: His abundance is like a curtain through which he can see the Pole Star at midday. He meets his lord and they are alike. There will be good fortune.

Fifth line Yin: His inner brilliance wins honour and praise. Auspicious.

Top line Yin: Enormous palace, shaded home. Peek in at the door – it is silent and unoccupied. No one is seen there for three years.

HEXAGRAM 56

Be humble on the road.

First line Yin: The traveller is engaged in worthless activities and exhausts himself.

Second line Yin: The traveller arrives at an inn, carrying his goods. He obtains the services of a loyal servant.

HEXAGRAM 56

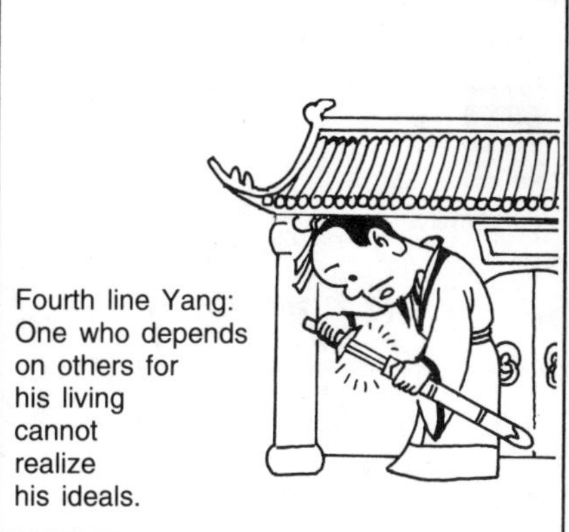

Third line Yang: The traveller burns down the inn. He loses his faithful servant. He is in danger if he remains as he is.

Fourth line Yang: The traveller finds shelter and has his goods with him. But his heart is not at ease.

Fifth line Yin: He shoots at a pheasant but his first arrow misses its mark. Eventually he is praised and given an official post.

Top line Yang: The bird's nest burns. The traveller's laughter turns into wailing. He loses an ox. There will be misfortune.

HEXAGRAM 57

Be yielding in small matters.

First line Yin: He advances and then retreats. It is helpful to be prepared like a soldier taking orders.

Second line Yang: He kneels before the royal couch. He is consecrated by the scribes and diviners. It is auspicious and he comes to no harm.

HEXAGRAM 57

Third line Yang: Do not think too long. Too much deliberation is procrastination.

Fourth line Yin: He carries out instructions and is rewarded.

Fifth line Yang: He is scrupulous and fair in his dealings and everything proceeds smoothly.

Top line Yang: The weakling loses his dignity.

Third line Yang: He is persistent but submissive. This is regrettable.

Fourth line Yin: There are no regrets. He catches three kinds of game while hunting.

Fifth line Yang: Proper behaviour brings good fortune. Regrets will pass. Everything he does is advantageous. The start may not be good but things will turn out well in the end. It bodes well to be careful before a change and reflective afterward.

Top line Yang: He kneels before the royal couch. He loses his possessions and his axe. There will be misfortune even if he is steadfast.

A time of joyous interaction.

Second line Yang: He is a man who abides by virtue. Temptations have no pull on him.

First line Yang: Happiness and harmony. There will be good fortune.

Second line Yang: Sincerity and happiness. There will be good fortune. Regret vanishes.

HEXAGRAM 58

Fifth line Yang: Be wary of petty people who have ulterior motives for associating with you. They are a corrupting influence.

Third line Yin: Happiness is forced. There will be misfortune.

Fourth line Yang: He deliberates about what will give him happiness but this does not satisfy him. Renounce this affliction and there will be rejoicing.

Fifth line Yang: He is confident despite the perils around him. This is dangerous.

Top line Yin: Seductive happiness.

HEXAGRAM 59

Huan

Your ego causes problems with others.

First line Yin: The horse used for rescue is strong. Auspicious.

Second line Yang: When there is dispersal, seek support and regret vanishes.

HEXAGRAM 59

Third line Yin: He disregards his own person. This is no cause for regret.

Fourth line Yin: He disperses the group. There will be good fortune. He scatters and then gathers in a mound.

Fifth line Yang: He is dripping with sweat when he calls out loudly. He has done nothing wrong. The king remains in spite of dispersion. There is no blame.

Top line Yang: He scatters his blood. He goes far away. There will be no mistakes.

HEXAGRAM 60

First line Yang: He does not go out of the courtyard outside his door. There will be no harm.

Second line Yang: He does not go out of the courtyard inside his gate. Inauspicious.

HEXAGRAM 60

Third line Yin: Lack of restraint brings lamentation but no harm.

Fourth line Yin: Stable restraint is auspicious.

Fifth line Yang: Strict restraint is auspicious. His advance is praised.

Top line Yin: Bitter restraint. To continue brings misfortune. Regrets will pass.

HEXAGRAM 61

First line Yang: Be careful about the kind of company you keep.

First line Yang: He is prepared. There will be good fortune. Otherwise he would be uneasy when the unexpected happens.

Second line Yang: A crane calls from her cover and its chick answers, "I have a fine goblet and I will drink with you."

HEXAGRAM 61

Third line Yin: He meets companions. He beats the drum and then stops. He weeps and then sings.

Fourth line Yin: The moon is almost full. The horse has lost its mate. No harm.

Fifth line Yang: Bound by allegiance to what is right, he comes to no harm.

Top line Yang: The cockerel tries to fly up to the sky. It is inauspicious to persist.

HEXAGRAM 62

Act with restraint and pay attention to small things.

First line Yin: The higher you go, the harder you fall.

Second line Yin: A slight excess is no bad thing.

First line Yin: The bird is on the wing. There will be misfortune.

Second line Yin: When you have passed the grandmother but meet the mother, or when you cannot reach the ruler but meet the minister, there will be no blame.

HEXAGRAM 62

Third line Yang: Try not to be too self-assured because you will make others jealous.

Fourth line Yang: Do not force yourself on others. Teach by example.

Fifth line Yin: He deviates from what is right.

Top line Yin: Your ambitions are too great and will lead to your downfall.

Third line Yang: He is attacked by pursuers because he is not sufficiently careful. There will be misfortune.

Fourth line Yang: No harm. Instead of passing by, he meets him. There is danger ahead, be on guard. Do not keep on as you are.

Fifth line Yin: There is a dense cloud which is coming from the western lands, but no rain. The duke shoots and takes the bird from the hole.

Top line Yin: He passes by without encounter. The bird that flies is netted. Misfortune. There will be disaster.

A phase of your life has reached a climax.

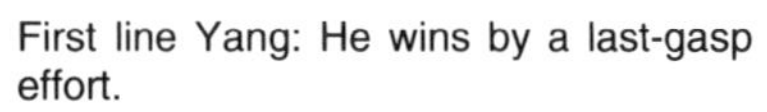

First line Yang: He wins by a last-gasp effort.

Second line Yin:
He rules without selfish motives.
There will be peace and stability.

First line Yang: The wheels of his carriage drag in the mud. The fox gets its tail wet. No harm.

Second line Yin: A wife loses her carriage curtain. She must not chase after it. In seven days she will get it back.

HEXAGRAM 63

Third line Yang: Be strong internally and externally so that peace will not be transient.

Fourth line Yin: Be prepared always and you will have no cause for regret.

Fifth line Yang: He lives it up for too long and degeneration sets in.

Top line Yin : Success turns into failure.

Third line Yang: The noble ancestor attacked a devilish territory but took three years to subdue it. Petty people are not to be employed.

Fourth line Yin: His padded jacket gets wet. He remains apprehensive all day.

Fifth line Yang: The eastern neighbour slaughters an ox, but his sacrifice does not bring as full a blessing as the western neighbour's modest offering.

Top line Yin: He gets his head wet. This is dangerous.

The goal is within reach but do not celebrate prematurely.

First line Yin: He is unaware of his limitations and puts himself at risk.

Second line Yang: He maintains his position and does not act rashly.

First line Yin: He gets his tail wet. There will be trouble.

Second line Yang: He puts the brakes on his wheels. Proper behaviour will bring good fortune.

HEXAGRAM 64

Third line Yin: He does not know what he is in for and acts recklessly.

Fourth line Yang: It is time to take action. Do not flinch.

Fifth line Yin: Work with people of calibre and success is within reach.

Top line Yang: He enjoys fame but success has its dangers. Pride goes before a fall.

Third line Yin: He advances and meets with misfortune before things are completed. It is favourable to cross a great river.

Fourth line Yang: Integrity bodes well. Regrets will pass. Stir into action to attack a devilish land, and in three years you will be rewarded with a great country.

Fifth line Yin: Integrity will bring good fortune. There is no cause for regret. He has the glory of the wise man and he is sincere. Auspicious.

Top line Yang: It is blameless to have faith in wine drinking, but if you get drunk it is no longer right to have such faith.

Divination Guidelines

1. You must be calm and collected when consulting the I Ching. Never attempt divination while in an agitated state of mind.

2. Make sure your hands are clean when consulting the I Ching. Keep the things you use for divination in a clean place. Do not share or let others handle the things you use for divination.

3. Ask only questions about important things. Do not ask question for fun.

4. Your question should be short and specific. For example:
   Should I do this?
   What will happen if I act in this way?
   What is the outcome of this plan?
   Make sure your question contains no ambiguity. Do not ask double questions, for example:
   Should I do this, and what will happen if I act in this way?
   Avoid questions requiring *Yes* or *No* answers.

5. If you prefer, you need not ask any question. The I Ching will respond to a major issue of your life and advise on the general situation.

6. Do not repeat the question. If an answer seems obscure, rephrase it and ask it again some other time.

7. Do not ask more than three questions a day. Consulting the I Ching is hard work and can cause a person to feel spiritually drained.

Hexagram Chart

Lower Trigram \ Upper Trigram	Qian ☰	Zhen ☳	Kan ☵	Gen ☶	Kun ☷	Xun ☴	Li ☲	Dui ☱
Qian ☰	1	34	5	26	11	9	14	43
Zhen ☳	25	51	3	27	24	42	21	17
Kan ☵	6	40	29	4	7	59	64	47
Gen ☶	33	62	39	52	15	53	56	31
Kun ☷	12	16	8	23	2	20	35	45
Xun ☴	44	32	48	18	46	57	50	28
Li ☲	13	55	63	22	36	37	30	49
Dui ☱	10	54	60	41	19	61	38	58

Additional Divination Methods

Besides the Yarrow Stalk Method, there are other methods of I Ching divination. They are as follows:

THREE COINS METHOD: Three coins are taken up and thrown down together, and each throw gives a line. Head counts as Yin, with a value of 2, and tail counts as Yang, with a value of 3. From this the character of the line is derived. Four combinations are possible. If all three coins are Yin, it is a 6 (changing line); if all three lines are Yang, the line is 9 (changing line). Two Yin and one Yang yield a 7, and two Yang and one Yin yield an 8.

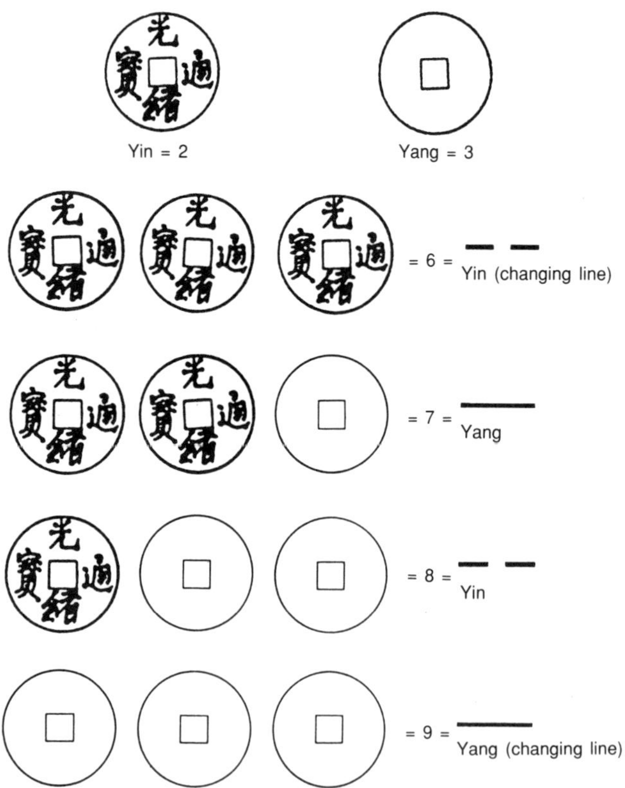

THE PEBBLE METHOD: Modern readers, who often feel that their time is limited, will find a suitable compromise in the Pebble Method. It takes a little longer than the Coin Method but not as long as the Yarrow Stalk Method. For this you need only one pebble that is fairly flat on both sides, more or less circular, about 3 cm in diameter and with rounded edges.

Mark one side of your pebble with two dots, the other with three dots. This can be done with a felt-tipped pen or with paint. To obtain your hexagram with the pebble, proceed as you did with the three coins. But instead of throwing three coins once for each line, you throw the pebble three times. Each throw will show either two dots or three. Write down the results of the three throws. This total tells you the number of the bottom line of your hexagram. If, for example, you threw : + : + :, the total would be six. Each total corresponds to a solid or broken line as follows:

6 — — x (changing line)
7 ———
8 — —
9 ——— x (changing line)

Build up the lines of the hexagram from the bottom up, by throwing the pebble three times for each line. In all, you will have thrown the pebble 18 times (3x6). Take your time and ponder over the question you would like to have answered while you keep adding the lines.

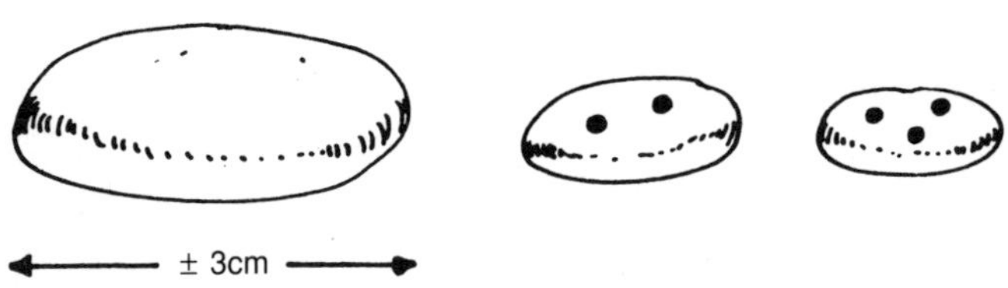

EIGHT COINS METHOD: For this method, the Fu Xi chart of the Eight Trigrams is used. Note that the Chinese, when setting out the cardinal points, always place south at the top. Eight coins of the same denomination are used. One of them should be marked in some way to differentiate it from the others.

The advantage of the Eight Coins Method is that there are no changing lines. The diviner is directed straightaway to the line of change from which he will read the divination.

The diviner mixes up the eight coins in his hands. He starts by placing a coin on the Qian trigram, the south one. Then he takes a second coin and places it on the Dui trigram, then on to Li and Zhen. If the marked coin has not come up yet, he goes on to Xun, Kan, Gen and finally, if necessary, to Kun.

If at any point the marked coin is placed upon a trigram, he stops, because that is the trigram which forms the bottom three lines of the hexagram which will provide the answer to his question.

For example, let us imagine the marked coin lands on Dui. This forms the bottom trigram of the hexagram. He now shuffles the coins again and repeats the process. Let us say the marked coin now lands on Li. This forms the upper trigram of the hexagram. The result is Hexagram 38. Having ascertained the hexagram it now remains to find the line of change which will give the answer to the diviner's question. To find the line of change, remove two unmarked coins from the eight. Then, mixing up the six coins as before, place them in an ascending line. Start at the bottom. When the marked coin appears, that is the line to refer to.

FU XI CHART OF THE EIGHT TRIGRAMS

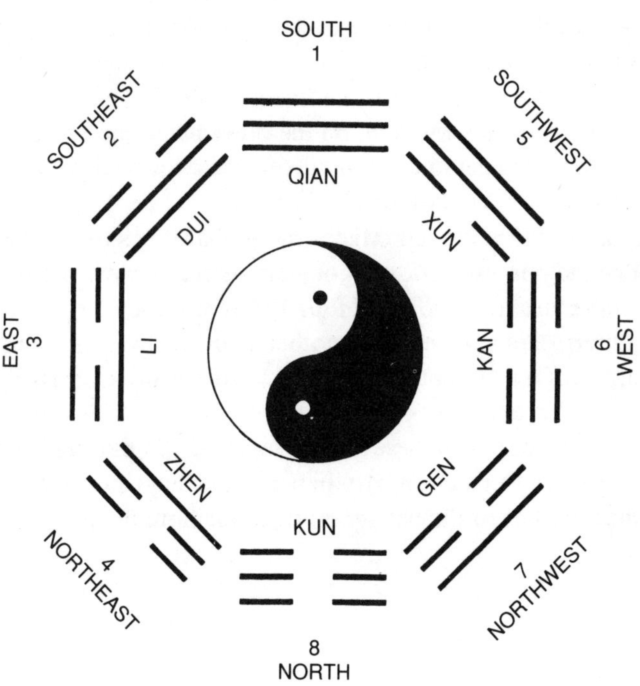

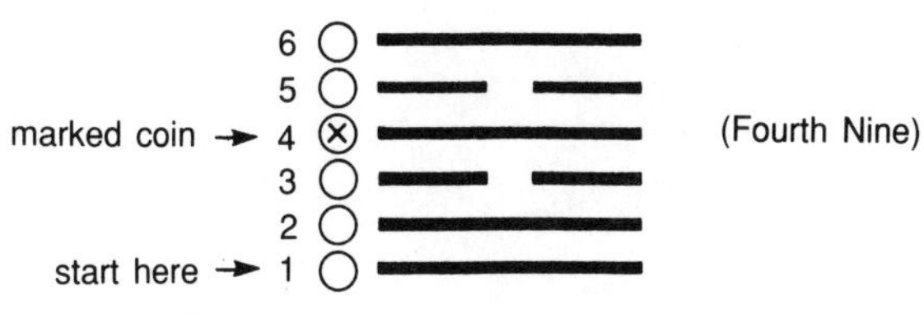

KUI (HEXAGRAM 38)

THE METHOD OF SIXTEEN: This is a new and simple method proposed by Larry Schoenholtz in his book, *New Directions in the I Ching.* Its main advantage is a statistical one. With the Yarrow Stalk Method, the probabilities of getting each of the four different kinds of lines are not the same: the chances of getting a broken line (8 — —) are 7 out of 16; the chances of getting a solid line (7 ——) are 5 out of 16; for a solid line that changes (9 —— x), they are 3 out of 16; for a broken line that changes (6 — — x), there is only 1 chance in 16.

With the Three Coins Method, on the other hand, the chances of getting either kind of unchanging lines are 6 out of 16 and those of getting either kind of changing lines are 2 out of 16.

The Method of Sixteen reproduces the probabilities of the Yarrow Stalk Method. The method uses 16 small objects such as beads, shells or pebbles, all of the same size and shape but of four different colours or patterns: 7 of one colour or pattern, 5 of another, 3 of another, and 1 of another. Each of the four groups represents a different kind of line: 7/16 = 8 — — , 5/16 = 7 —— , 3/16 = 9 —— x, 1/16 = 6 — — x.

Randomly choose one of these objects for each line, putting it back with the others (perhaps kept in a cloth bag) before choosing again for the next line. Build up the six lines of the hexagram from the bottom up.

A Brief Chronology of Chinese History

Dynasty / Period			Dates
夏 Xia Dynasty			About 2100 – 1600 BC
商 Shang Dynasty			About 1600 – 1100 BC
周 Zhou Dynasty	西周 Western Zhou Dynasty		About 1100 – 771 BC
	東周 Eastern Zhou Dynasty		770 – 256 BC
	春秋 Spring and Autumn Period		770 – 476 BC
	戰國 Warring States		475 – 221 BC
秦 Qin Dynasty			221 – 207 BC
漢 Han Dynasty	西漢 Western Han		206 BC – AD 24
	東漢 Eastern Han		25 – 220
三國 Three Kingdoms	魏 Wei		220 – 265
	蜀漢 Shu Han		221 – 263
	吳 Wu		222 – 280
西晋 Western Jin Dynasty			265 – 316
東晋 Eastern Jin Dynasty			317 – 420
南北朝 Northern and Southern Dynasties	南朝 Southern Dynasties	宋 Song	420 – 479
		齊 Qi	479 – 502
		梁 Liang	502 – 557
		陳 Chen	557 – 589
	北朝 Northern Dynasties	北魏 Northern Wei	386 – 534
		東魏 Eastern Wei	534 – 550
		北齊 Northern Qi	550 – 577
		西魏 Western Wei	535 – 556
		北周 Northern Zhou	557 – 581
隋 Sui Dynasty			581 – 618
唐 Tang Dynasty			618 – 907
五代 Five Dynasties	後梁 Later Liang		907 – 923
	後唐 Later Tang		923 – 936
	後晋 Later Jin		936 – 946
	後漢 Later Han		947 – 950
	後周 Later Zhou		951 – 960
宋 Song Dynasty	北宋 Northern Song Dynasty		960 – 1127
	南宋 Southern Song Dynasty		1127 – 1279
遼 Liao Dynasty			916 – 1125
金 Jin Dynasty			1115 – 1234
元 Yuan Dynasty			1271 – 1368
明 Ming Dynasty			1368 – 1644
清 Qing Dynasty			1644 – 1911
中華民國 Republic of China			1912 – 1949
中華人民共和國 People's Republic of China			1949 –

Further Reading

1. John Blofeld, *I Ching*, Allen and Unwin, 1964.
Also available in Mandala paperback.
This book offers a good introduction to the I Ching for those who know nothing about it.

2. Thomas Cleary, *I Ching: The Tao of Organization*, Shambala.
The author has also translated a pocket-size *I Ching, Taoist I Ching, Buddhist I Ching* and *I Ching*, Mandalas (all published by Shambala).

3. Anthony Clark and Richard Gill, *The I Ching Pack*, The Aquarian Press, 1993.
Innovative method of divination using a pack of cards.

4. Da Liu, *T'ai Chi Ch'uan and I Ching*, Harper and Row, 1972.
Also available in Arkana paperback.

5. Guy Damian-Knight, *The I Ching on Love*, Blandford Press, 1984.

6. Alfred Douglas, *The Oracle of Change*, Gollancz, 1971.

7. Peter Hazel, *Ancient Chinese I Ching*, Lothian Publishing Company.
Also published by Pelanduk Publications, 1991.

8. Kerson Huang, *I Ching: The Oracle*, World Scientific Pub. Co., 1984.
A computer programme of the I Ching is available from the author.

9. Christopher Markert, *I Ching: The No. 1 Success Formula*, The Aquarian Press, 1986.
Misleading title. This book looks at the I Ching from a philosophical viewpoint.

10. Gary Melyan and Wen-kuang Chu, *The Pocket I Ching*, Yenbooks by Charles E. Tuttle Co. Inc., 1988.
Unusual presentation of the I Ching on how it applies to specific situations.

11. Martin Palmer, Kwok Man Ho and Joanne O'Brien, *The Fortune Teller's I Ching*, Ballantine Books, 1987.
Also published as *The Contemporary I Ching* by Rider.

12. Larry Schoenholtz, *New Directions in the I Ching*, University Books, 1975.

13. W.A. Sherrill and W.K. Chu, *Astrology of the I Ching*, Routledge and Keegan Paul, 1975.
See also *An Anthology of the I Ching*, Arkana, 1977.

14. Diane Stein, *The Kwan Yin Book of Changes*, Llewellyn Publications, 1985.
Interpretation of the I Ching from a woman's viewpoint.

15. John Tampion, Maureen Tampion, Karen Hughes and Judy Fox, *An Illuminated I Ching*, Prentice Hall Press, 1988.

16. Henry Wei, *The Authentic I Ching: A New Translation with Commentary*, Borgo Press, Newcastle Publishing Co., 1987.

17. Greg Whincup, *Rediscovering the I Ching*, Doubleday, 1986.
This book purports to present the I Ching in its original form.

18. Richard Wilhelm, *The I Ching or Book of Changes*, first published in German in 1924, English translation in 1950, Arkana.

19. Ann Williams, Images from the I Ching's visual meditations on the Book of Change, Craftsman House, 1987.
A book of paintings on the hexagrams.

20. R.L. Wing, *The Illustrated I Ching*, Dolphin Book, 1982.
The I Ching Workbook, The Aquarian Press, 1983.

Forthcoming...

(*100 Series* Art Album)

Forthcoming...

(Asiapac Comic Series)

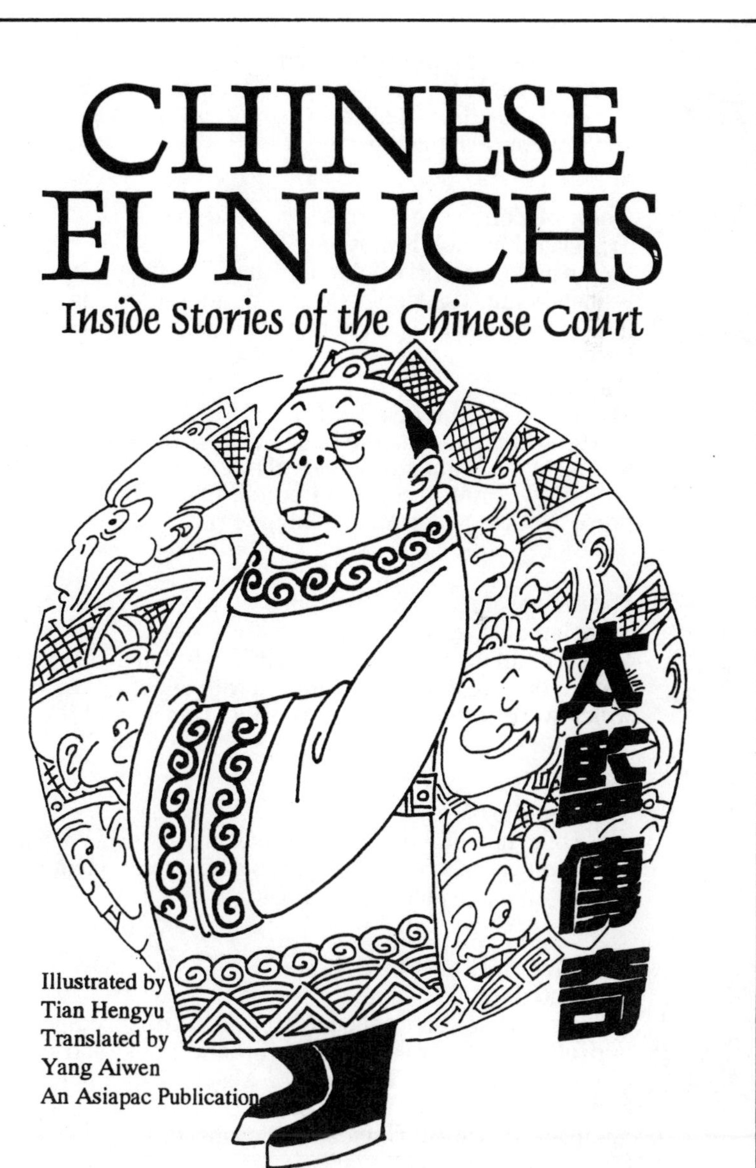

Asiapac Comic Series (by Tsai Chih Chung)

Art of War
Translated by Leong Weng Kam
The Art of War provides a compact set of principles essential for victory in battles; applicable to military strategists, in business and human relationships.

Book of Zen
Translated by Koh Kok Kiang
Zen makes the art of spontaneous living the prime concern of the human being. Tsai depicts Zen with unfettered versatility; his illustrations spans a period of more than 2,000 years.

Da Xue
Translated by Mary Ng En Tzu
The second book in the Four Books of the Confucian Classics. It sets forth the higher principles of moral science and advocates that the cultivation of the person be the first thing attended to in the process of the pacification of kingdoms.

Fantasies of the Six Dynasties
Translated by Jenny Lim
Tsai Chih Chung has creatively illustrated and annotated 19 bizarre tales of human encounters with supernatural beings which were compiled during the Six Dyansties (AD 220-589).

Lun Yu
Translated by Mary Ng En Tzu
A collection of the discourses of Confucius, his disciples and others on various topics. Several bits of choice sayings have been illustrated for readers in this book.

New Account of World Tales
Translated by Alan Chong
These 120 selected anecdotes tell the stories of emperors, princes, high officials, generals, courtiers, urbane monks and lettered gentry of a turbulent time. They afford a stark and amoral insight into human behaviour in its full spectrum of virtues and frailties and glimpses of brilliant Chinese witticisms, too.

Origins of Zen
Translated by Koh Kok Kiang
Tsai in this book traces the origins and development of Zen in China with a light-hearted touch which is very much in keeping with the Zen spirit of absolute freedom and unbounded creativity.

Records of the Historian
Translated by Tang Nguok Kiong
Adapted from Records of the Historian, one of the greatest historical work China has produced, Tsai has illustrated the life and characteristics of the Four Lords of the Warring Strates.

Roots of Wisdom
Translated by Koh Kok Kiang
One of the gems of Chinese literature, whose advocacy of a steadfast nature and a life of simplicity, goodness, quiet joy and harmony with one's fellow beings and the world at large has great relevance in an age of rapid changes.

Sayings of Confucius
Translated by Goh Beng Choo
This book features the life of Confucius, selected sayings from The Analects and some of his more prominent pupils. It captures the warm relationship between the sage and his disciples, and offers food for thought for the modern readers.

Sayings of Han Fei Zi
Translated by Alan Chong
Tsai Chih Chung retold and interpreted the basic ideas of legalism, a classical political philosophy that advocates a draconian legal code, embodying a system of liberal reward and heavy penalty as the basis of government, in his unique style.

Sayings of Lao Zi
Translated by Koh Kok Kiang & Wong Lit Khiong
The thoughts of Lao Zi, the founder of Taoism, are presented here in a light-hearted manner. It features the selected sayings from Dao De Jing.

Sayings of Lao Zi Book 2
Translated by Koh Kok Kiang

In the second book, Tsai Chih Chung has tackled some of the more abstruse passages from the Dao De Jing which he has not included in the first volume of Sayings of Lao Zi.

Sayings of Lie Zi
Translated by Koh Kok Kiang

A famous Taoist sage whose sayings deals with universal themes such as the joy of living, reconciliation with death, the limitations of human knowledge, the role of chance events.

Sayings of Mencius
Translated by Mary Ng En Tzu

This book contains stories about the life of Mencius and various excerpts from "Mencius", one of the Four Books of the Confucian Classics, which contains the philosophy of Mencius.

Sayings of Zhuang Zi
Translated by Goh Beng Choo

Zhuang Zi's non-conformist and often humorous views of life have been creatively illustrated and simply presented by Tsai Chih Chung in this book.

Sayings of Zhuang Zi Book 2
Translated by Koh Kok Kiang

Zhuang Zi's book is valued for both its philosophical insights and as a work of great literary merit. Tsai's second book on Zhuang Zi shows maturity in his unique style.

Strange Tales of Liaozhai
Translated by Tang Nguok Kiong

In this book, Tsai Chih Chung has creatively illustrated 12 stories from the Strange Tales of Liaozhai, an outstanding Chinese classic written by Pu Songling in the early Qing Dynasty.

Zhong Yong
Translated by Mary Ng En Tzu

Zhong Yong, written by Zi Si, the grandson of Confucius, gives voice to the heart of the discipline of Confucius. Tsai has presented it in a most readable manner for the modern readers to explore with great delight.

Hilarious Chinese Classics by Tsai Chih Chung

Journey to the West 1

These books offer more than the all-too-familiar escapades of Tan Sanzang and his animal disciples. Under the creative pen of Tsai Chih Chung, *Journey to the West* still stays its course but takes a new route. En route from ancient China to India to acquire Buddhist scriptures, the Monk and his disciples veer off course frequently to dart into modern times to have fleeting exchanges with characters ranging from Ronald Reagan to Bunny Girls of the Playboy Club.

Journey to the West 2

Romance of the Three Kingdoms

Set in the turbulent Three Kingdoms Period, *Romance of the Three Kingdoms* relates the clever political manoeuvres and brilliant battle strategies used by the ambitious rulers as they fought one another for supremacy.

In this comic version, Tsai Chih Chung has illustrated in an entertaining way the four best-known episodes in the novel. Don't be surprised to see a warrior waving an Iraqi flag, a satellite dish fixed on top of an ancient Chinese building, and court officials playing mahjong or eating beef noodles, a favourite Taiwanese snack.

Strategy & Leadership Series by Wang Xuanming

Thirty-six Stratagems: Secret Art of War
Translated by Koh Kok Kiang (cartoons) &
Liu Yi (text of the stratagems)

A Chinese military classic which emphasizes deceptive schemes to achieve military objectives. It has attracted the attention of military authorities and general readers alike.

Six Strategies for War: The Practice of Effective Leadership
Translated by Alan Chong

A powerful book for rulers, administrators and leaders, it covers critical areas in management and warfare including: how to recruit talents and manage the state; how to beat the enemy and build an empire; how to lead wisely; and how to manoeuvre brilliantly.

Gems of Chinese Wisdom: Mastering the Art of Leadership
Translated by Leong Weng Kam

Wise up with this delightful collection of tales and anecdotes on the wisdom of great men and women in Chinese history, including Confucius, Meng Changjun and Gou Jian.

Three Strategies of Huang Shi Gong: The Art of Government
Translated by Alan Chong

Reputedly one of man's oldest monograph on military strategy, it unmasks the secrets behind brilliant military manoeuvres, clever deployment and control of subordinates, and effective government.

100 Strategies of War: Brilliant Tactics in Action
Translated by Yeo Ai Hoon

The book captures the essence of extensive military knowledge and practice, and explores the use of psychology in warfare, the importance of building diplomatic relations with the enemy's neighbours, the use of espionage and reconnaissance, etc.

Latest Titles in Asiapac Comic Series

Battle Domestica

A satire about married life typified by a middle-aged couple who derive sadistic pleasure from mutual verbal assault.

Known as *Double Big Guns* in Taiwan, its Chinese edition has sold more than 400,000 copies worldwide.

Sour Pack

There exist among us people who participate but are never committed; who are willing to give but attach more importance to what they get in return; who long for love but are terrified of being tied down.

Images of these people, their credo, and their lifestyles are reflected in the book. You may find in these cartoon characters familiar glimpses of yourself or those around you.

《亞太漫畫系列》

易經

編繪：譚曉春
翻譯：許國強

亞太圖書有限公司出版